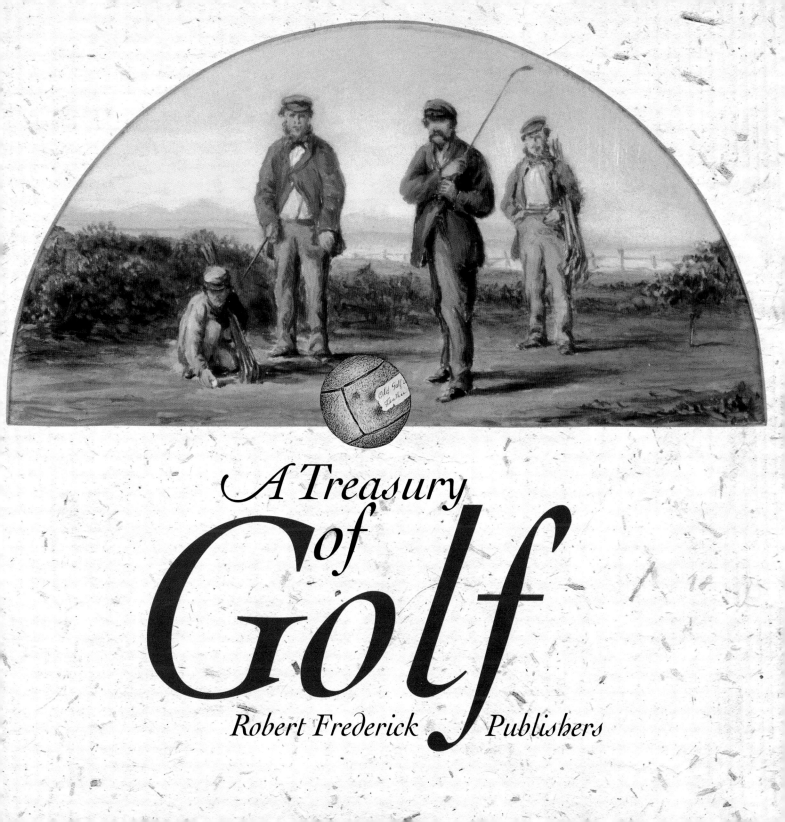

# A Treasury
## of
# Golf

Robert Frederick  Publishers

PHOTOGRAPHIC
ACKNOWLEDGEMENTS
Colour images, including
front cover, courtesy of
**Allsport**-Photographers:
David Cannon,
David Duval, Matthew
Stockman, Stephen Munday,
Steve Powell, Rusty Jarrett,
Andrew Redington

This collection
© Robert Frederick
Publishers
First edition 2000
4 & 5 North Parade
Bath
England

# Contents

# A *definition, circa* 1900

**Golf**, A GAME PLAYED with clubs and balls, generally over large commons, downs, or links, where a series of small round holes are cut in the turf at distances of from 100 to 500 yards from each other, according to the nature of the ground, so as to form a circuit or round. The clubs are of different uses, and have  different names according to the purpose for which they are respectively designed; as the *driver, putter, brassey, mashie, cleck, iron, niblick,* etc. The rival players are one on each side, or  two against two, in which case the two partners strike the ball on their side alternately. The object of the game is, starting from the first hole, to drive the ball into the next hole with as few strokes as possible, and so on with all the holes in succession, the side which 'holes' its ball on any occasion with the fewest strokes being said to gain the hole. The match is usually decided by the greatest number of holes gained in one or more rounds, or the aggregate number of strokes taken to hole one or more rounds. In medal play the score is always reckoned by strokes. Golf, which was long almost entirely confined to Scotland, is now established in England and elsewhere.

A golf course is the epitome of all that is purely transitory in the universe, a space not to dwell in, but to get over as quickly as possible.

*Jean Giraudoux*

"I never pray on the golf course. Actually, the Lord answers my prayers everywhere except on the course."

*Billy Graham*

He's hit it fat. . . . It will probably be short. . . . It just hit the front edge of the green. . . . It's got no chance. . . . It's rolling but it will stop. . . . It's rolling toward the cup. . . . Well, I'll be damned!

*Jimmy Demaret (commentating at the World Championship in 1953 on Lew Worsham's winning wedge shot)*

My game is so bad I gotta hire three caddies - one to walk the left rough, one for the right rough, and one down the middle. And the one in the middle doesn't have much to do.

*Dave Hillu*

At my first Masters, I got the feeling that if I didn't play well, I wouldn't go to heaven.

*Dave Marr*

# Famous Golfing Quotations

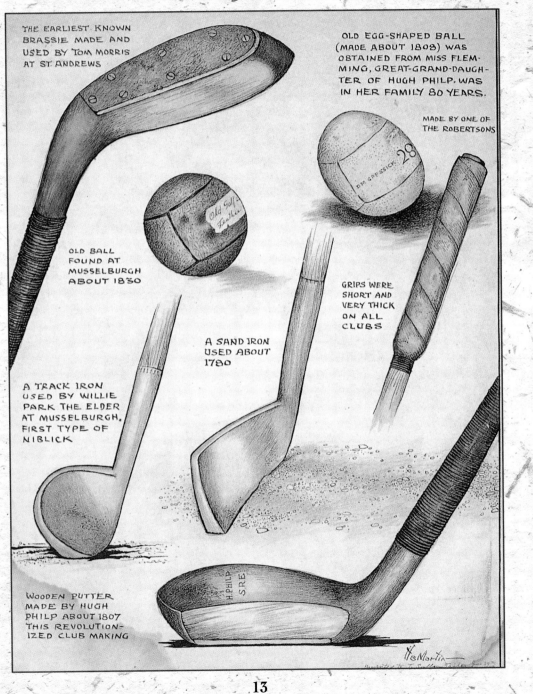

THE EARLIEST KNOWN BRASSIE MADE AND USED BY TOM MORRIS AT ST. ANDREWS

OLD EGG-SHAPED BALL (MADE ABOUT 1808) WAS OBTAINED FROM MISS FLEMMING, GREAT-GRAND-DAUGHTER OF HUGH PHILP. WAS IN HER FAMILY 80 YEARS.

MADE BY ONE OF THE ROBERTSONS

OLD BALL FOUND AT MUSSELBURGH ABOUT 1830

GRIPS WERE SHORT AND VERY THICK ON ALL CLUBS

A SAND IRON USED ABOUT 1780

A TRACK IRON USED BY WILLIE PARK THE ELDER AT MUSSELBURGH, FIRST TYPE OF NIBLICK

WOODEN PUTTER MADE BY HUGH PHILP ABOUT 1807 THIS REVOLUTIONIZED CLUB MAKING

Never give up.  If we give up in this game, we'll give up on life.  If you give up that first time, its' easier to give up the second, third, and fourth times.

*Tom Watson*

Golf is deceptively simple, endlessly complicated.  A child can play it well and a grown man can never master it.  It is almost a science, yet a puzzle with no answer.

*Arnold Palmer*

I have found, in my own matches, that if you just keep throwing consistent, unvarying bogeys and double bogeys at your opponents, they will crack up sooner or later from the pressure.

*Rex Lardner*

One reason golf is such an exasperating game is that a thing learned is so easily forgotten and we find ourselves struggling year after year with faults we had discovered and corrected time and time again.

*Robert T. 'Bobby' Jones*

$M$y golf swing is like ironing a shirt. You get one side smoothed out, turn it over and there is a big wrinkle on the other side. You iron that side, turn it over and there's another wrinkle.

*Tom Watson*

$T$he vital thing about a hole is that it should either be more difficult than it looks or look more difficult than it is. It must never be what it looks.

*Sir Walter Simpson*

Thou shalt not use profanity; thou shalt not covet thy neighbour's putter; thou shalt not steal thy neighbour's ball; thou shalt not bear false witness in the final tally.

*Ground Rules: Clergyman's Golf Tournament, Grand Rapids*

**A**ll games are silly, but golf, if you look at it dispassionately, goes to extremes.

*Peter Alliss*

**W**hat's over there? A nudist colony?

*Lee Trevino (after his 3 playing partners drove into the woods)*

All I have against it is that it takes you so far from the clubhouse

*Eric Linklater*

Golf is a game in which a ball - one and a half inches in diameter - is placed on a ball - 8,000 miles in diameter.  The object being to hit the small ball, but not the larger.

*John Cunningham*

A Scotsman is the only golfer not trying to hit the ball out of sight.

*Anon*

You hit the ball and if it doesn't go far enough you just hit it again, and if that doesn't work, you hit it again, and so on.

*Robert Robinson*

## Golf is a good walk spoiled.
*Mark Twain*

Anytime you get the urge to golf, instead take 18 minutes and beat your head against a good solid wall!  This is guaranteed to duplicate to a tee the physical and emotional beating you would have suffered playing a round of golf.  If 18 minutes aren't enough, go for 27 or 36 - whatever feels right.

*Mark Oman*

$A$s of this writing, there are approximately 2,450 reasons why a person hits a rotten shot, and more are being discovered every day.

*Jay Cronley*

$W$hen ground rules permit a golfer to improve his lie, he can either move his ball or change the story about his score.

*Anon*

There's only one thing wrong about Babe and me.  I hit like a girl and she hits like a man.

*Bob Hope (referring to Babe Didrikson Zaharias)*

My goal this year is basically to find the fairways.

*Lauri Peterson*

When he gets the ball into a tough place, that's when he's most relaxed. I think it's because he has so much experience at it.

*Don Christopher*
*(Jack Lemon's*
*caddie)*

Anytime a golfer hits a ball perfectly straight with a big club it is, in my view, a fluke.

*Jack Nicklaus*

Most golfers prepare for disaster. A good golfer prepares for success.

*Bob Toski*

Suffering - ! I've got a hen back home in Charlotte that can lay an egg further than that!

*Clayton Heafner, (missing a 3 inch putt to lose the Oakland Open by one shot)*

I visualise hitting the ball as far as JoAnne Carner, putting like Amy Alcott, looking like Jan Stephenson and having Carol Mann's husband.

*Dinah Shore*

You've got to turn yourself into a material as soft as putty, and then just sort of slop the clubhead through. You'll hit much farther and with less effort.

*Johnny Miller*

If ah didn't have these ah'd hit it twenty yards further.

*Babe Didrikson Zaharias (referring to her breasts)*

He quit playing when I started outdriving him.

*JoAnne Carner (referring to her husband Don)*

PHILOSOPHER (*eight down to bogey*). "Anyway I don't suppose for one moment the cup is real silver."

Real golfers tape The Masters so they can go play themselves.

*George W Roope*

Everybody has two swings - a beautiful practice swing and a choked-up one with which they hit the ball. So it wouldn't do either of us a damned bit of good to look at your practice swing.

*Ed Furgol*

I don't think that was me that shot that eighty-four.  It must have been somebody else.  Actually, I was trying to get my handicap squared away.

*Fuzzy Zoeller*

Through years of experience I have found that air offers less resistance than dirt.

*Jack Nicklaus explaining why he tees up the ball so high*

Golf appeals to the idiot in us and the child . . . Just how childlike golf players become is proven by their frequent inability to count past five.

*John Updike*

Well, in plain old English, I'm driving it bad, chipping bad, putting bad, and not scoring at all. Other than that, and the fact I got up this morning, I guess everything's okay.

*Bob Wynn*

Whether a putter is waiting his turn to
hole-out a putt of one or two feet in
length, on which the match hangs at
the last hole, it is of vital importance
that he think of nothing.  At this
supreme moment he ought studiously
to fill his mind with vacancy.  He must
not even allow himself the consolation
of religion.

*Sir Walter G Simpson*

Keep on hitting it straight until the wee
ball goes in the hall.

*James Braid*

My caddie had the best answer to that
- 'Just to let the other one know it can
be replaced.'

*Larry Nelson explaining why he carried two putters*

J.V. McFALL
1903

Copyright 1903, by J Ellsworth Gross

Golf increases the blood pressure, ruins the disposition, spoils the digestion, induces neurasthenia, hurts the eyes, callouses the hands, ties kinks in the nervous system, debauches the morals, drives men to drink or homicide, breaks up the family, turns the ductless glands into internal warts, corrodes the pneumo-gastric nerve, breaks off the edges of the vertebrae, induces spinal meningitis and progressive mendacity, and starts angina pectoris.

*Dr. A S Lamb*

My Handicap?: Woods and irons.

*Chris Codiroli*

Over the years, I've studied habits of golfers. I know what to look for. Watch their eyes. Fear shows up when there is an enlargement of the pupils. Big pupils lead to big scores.

*Sam Snead*

If a ball comes to rest in dangerous proximity to a hippopotamus or crocodile, another ball may be dropped at a safe distance, no nearer the hole, without penalty.

*Local Rule: Nyanza Club, British East Africa
in the 1950s*

Real golfers don't cry when they line up their fourth putt.

*Karen Hurwitz*

He enjoys that perfect peace, that peace beyond all understanding, which comes at its maximum only to the man who has given up golf.

*P G Wodehouse*

A golf game doesn't end until
the last putt drops.

*Cary Middlecoff*

When Nicklaus plays well he wins,
when he plays badly he comes
second.  When he's playing terribly,
he's third.

*Johnny Miller*

The nice thing about these [golf] books is that they usually cancel each other out. One book tells you to keep your eye on the ball; the next says not to bother. Personally, in the crowd I play with, a better idea is to keep your eye on your partner.

*Jim Murray*

You've just one problem. You stand too close to the ball - after you've hit it.

*Sam Snead (to a pupil)*

Sure, the purses are obscene. The average worker, let's say, makes $25,000 a year, while a golfer makes $25,000 for finishing 10th. Our values have departed somewhat.

*Tom Watson (1989)*

Always throw clubs ahead of you. That way you don't have to waste energy going back to pick them up.

*Tommy Bolt*

The average expert player - if he is lucky - hits six, eight or ten real shots in a round.  The rest are good misses.

*Tommy Armour*

It is nothing new or original to say that golf is played one stroke at a time.  But it took me many years to realise it.

*Bobby Jones*

I always keep a supply of stimulants handy in case I see a snake, which I also keep handy.

*W C Fields (putting whisky in his golf bag)*

What the nineteenth hole proves beyond a shadow of a doubt is that the Scots invented the game solely in order to sell their national beverage in large quantities.

*Milton Gross*

Play is conducted at a snail's pace.
Some golfers today remind me of kids
walking to school and praying they'll be
late. . . . Golfers used to check the grass
of the greens; today they study the roots
under each blade.

*Jimmy Demaret (1954)*

Golf acts as a corrective against sinful pride. I attribute the insane arrogance of the later Roman emperors almost entirely to the fact that, never having played golf, they never knew that strange chastening humility which is engendered by a topped chip shot.

*P G Wodehouse*

I was afraid to move my lips in front of TV. The Commissioner probably would have fined me just for what I was thinking.

*Tom Weiskopf (on his 13 in the 1980 Masters)*

Everyone gets wounded in a game of golf. The trick is not to bleed.

*Peter Dobereiner*

If you keep shooting par at them, they all crack up sooner or later.

*Bobby Jones*

A secret disbelief in the enemy's play is very useful for match play.

*Sir Walter Simpson*

A good player who is a great putter is a match for any golfer.  A great hitter who cannot putt is a match for no one.

*Ben Sayers (1890s)*

Fairway: A narrow strip of mown grass that separates two groups of golfers looking for lost balls in the rough.

*Henry Beard & Roy McKie*

If the tree is skinny, aim right at it.  A peculiarity of golf is that what you aim at you generally miss,  . . . the success of the shot depending mainly, of course, on your definition of 'skinny.'

*Rex Lardner*

The fundamental problem with golf is that every so often, no matter how lacking you may be in the essential virtues required of a steady player, the odds are that one day you will hit the ball straight, hard and out of sight.  This is the essential frustration of this excruciating sport.  For when you've done it once, you make the fundamental error of asking yourself why you can't do it all the time.  The answer to this question is simple: the first time was a fluke.

*Colin Bowles*

President Ford waits until he hits his first drive to know what course he's playing that day.

*Bob Hope*

The difference between golf and government is that in golf you can't improve your lie.

*George Deukmejian (Governor of California)*

The golfer has more enemies than any other athlete.  He has 14 clubs in his bag, all of them different; 18 holes to play, all of them different, every week; and all around him are sand, trees, grass, water, wind and 143 other players.  In addition, the game is fifty percent mental, so his biggest enemy is himself.

*Dan Jenkins*

No man has mastered golf until he has realised that his good shots are accidents and his bad shots good exercise.

*Eugene R Black*

You get to know more of the character of a man in a round of golf than you can get to know in six months with only political experience.

*David Lloyd George*

Arnold Palmer had everything except a brake pedal.

*Peter Dobereiner*

He hits it in the woods so often he should get an orange hunting jacket.

*Tom Weiskopf on Ben Crenshaw*

Hole-in-One: An occurrence in which a ball is hit directly from the tee into the hole on a single shot by a golfer playing alone.

*Henry Beard & Roy McKie*

HEART-BROKEN COMPETITOR (*who has missed a quick putt*). "Now wouldn't you call that provoking?"
CADDIE. "Well, Miss, that's a word I don't use meself."

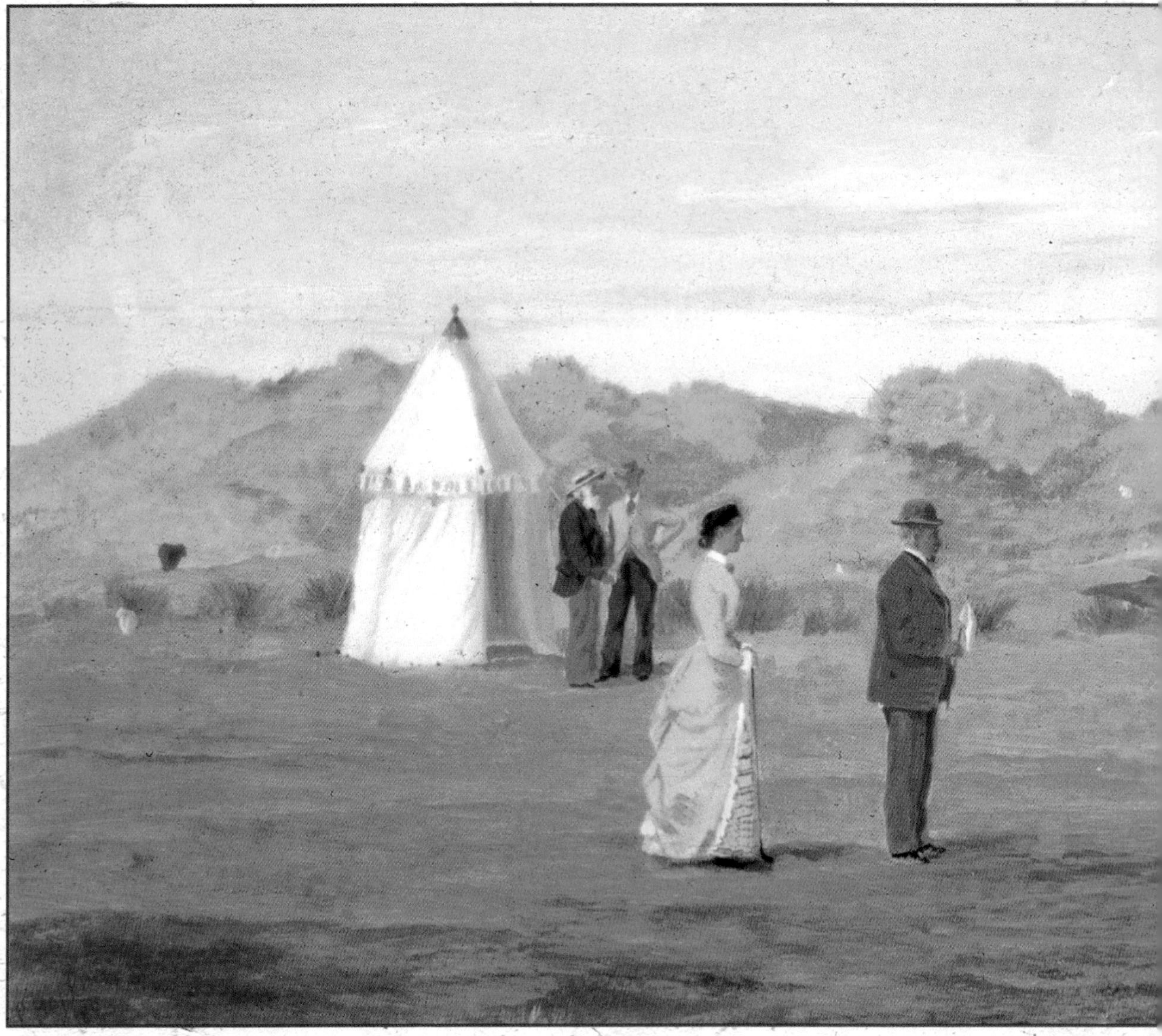

It is a strange thing that we know just how to do a thing at golf, and yet we cannot do it.

*Bernard Darwin*

I said to the writers, 'There's Nicklaus, for example, only five strokes back. I wouldn't feel safe from Jack if he was in a wheelchair.'

*Dan Jenkins*

Playing against him [Gary Player], you begin hoping he'll be on grass rather than in sand. From grass you expect him to pitch the ball close. From a bunker you're afraid he'll hole it out!

*Jack Nicklaus*

Only religious ceremonies proceed with more respect than the major golf tournaments in this country.

*Jimmy Cannon*

Tom Watson scares me.  If he's lying six in the middle of the fairway, there's some kind of way he might make a five.

*Lee Trevino*

The trouble with this game is that they say the good breaks and bad breaks even up.  What they don't tell you is that they don't even up right away.  You might go two or three years and all you get is bad-break bad-break bad-break.  That gets annoying in a hurry.

*Johnny Miller*

There are now more golf clubs in the world than Gideon Bibles, more golf balls than missionaries and, if every golfer in the world, male and or female, were laid end to end, I for one would leave them there.

*Michael Parkinson*

MEMBER (*describing his match to Club Professional*). "It was ding-dong the whole way round and I should never have lost but at the 18th he sprung a seven on me."

I'd like to see the fairways more narrow. Then everybody would have to play from the rough, not just me.

*Severiano Ballesteros*

The only difference between an amateur and a pro is that we call a shot that goes left-to-right a fade and an amateur calls it a slice.

*Peter Jacobsen*

I remember being upset once and telling my Dad I wasn't following through right, and he replied, 'Nancy, it doesn't make any difference to a ball what you do after you hit it.'

*Nancy Lopez*

The person I fear most in the last two round is myself.

*Tom Watson (at the US Open)*

The little white ball won't move until you've hit it, and there's nothing you can do after
it has gone.

*Babe Didrikson Zaharias*

Stroke play is a better test of golf, but match play is a better test of character.

*Joe Carr*

Golf is a typical capitalist lunacy of upper-class Edwardian England.

*George Bernard Shaw*

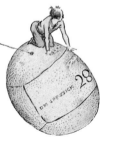

Water creates a neurosis in golfers. The very thought of this harmless fluid robs them of their normal powers of rational thought, turns their legs to jelly, and produces a palsy of the upper limbs.

*Peter Dobereiner*

He goes after a golf course like a lion at a zebra. He doesn't reason with it; he tries to throw it out of the window or hold its head under water till it stops wriggling.

*Jim Murray on Seve Ballesteros*

THE DUD WHO MISSED EVERYTHING

# Some famous Golfers

*&*

# Golfing Records

*Use the following section to record*

*your own, or your favourite personalities'*

*most memorable games.*

# *Golfing Records*

Course ...................................................... Date ...................................

Competition ..........................................................................................

Players

| Hole | Yards | Par | Self | Opponent |
|------|-------|-----|------|----------|
| 1 | | | | |
| 2 | | | | |
| 3 | | | | |
| 4 | | | | |
| 5 | | | | |
| 6 | | | | |
| 7 | | | | |
| 8 | | | | |
| 9 | | | | |
| Out | | | | |

| Hole | Yards | Par | Self | Opponent |
|------|-------|-----|------|----------|
| 10 | | | | |
| 11 | | | | |
| 12 | | | | |
| 13 | | | | |
| 14 | | | | |
| 15 | | | | |
| 16 | | | | |
| 17 | | | | |
| 18 | | | | |
| In | | | | |
| Out | | | | |
| Total | | | | |
| Handicap | | | | |
| Net Score | | | | |

Competitor's
Signature ................................................

Marker's
Signature ................................................

# Golfing Records

Course ........................................................... Date ...............................

Competition ...................................................................................

Players

| Hole | Yards | Par | Self | Opponent |
|------|-------|-----|------|----------|
| 1 | | | | |
| 2 | | | | |
| 3 | | | | |
| 4 | | | | |
| 5 | | | | |
| 6 | | | | |
| 7 | | | | |
| 8 | | | | |
| 9 | | | | |
| Out | | | | |

| Hole | Yards | Par | Self | Opponent |
|------|-------|-----|------|----------|
| 10 | | | | |
| 11 | | | | |
| 12 | | | | |
| 13 | | | | |
| 14 | | | | |
| 15 | | | | |
| 16 | | | | |
| 17 | | | | |
| 18 | | | | |
| In | | | | |
| Out | | | | |
| Total | | | | |
| Handicap | | | | |
| Net Score | | | | |

Competitor's
Signature ......................................................

Marker's
Signature ......................................................

# Golfing Records

Course ........................................................ Date ........................................

Competition ........................................................................................

Players

| Hole | Yards | Par | Self | Opponent |
|------|-------|-----|------|----------|
| 1 | | | | |
| 2 | | | | |
| 3 | | | | |
| 4 | | | | |
| 5 | | | | |
| 6 | | | | |
| 7 | | | | |
| 8 | | | | |
| 9 | | | | |
| Out | | | | |

| Hole | Yards | Par | Self | Opponent |
|------|-------|-----|------|----------|
| 10 | | | | |
| 11 | | | | |
| 12 | | | | |
| 13 | | | | |
| 14 | | | | |
| 15 | | | | |
| 16 | | | | |
| 17 | | | | |
| 18 | | | | |
| In | | | | |
| Out | | | | |
| Total | | | | |
| Handicap | | | | |
| Net Score | | | | |

Competitor's
Signature ........................................................

Marker's
Signature ........................................................

# *Golfing Records*

Course .................................................... Date ...........................

Competition ...................................................................................

Players

| Hole | Yards | Par | Self | Opponent |
|------|-------|-----|------|----------|
| 1 | | | | |
| 2 | | | | |
| 3 | | | | |
| 4 | | | | |
| 5 | | | | |
| 6 | | | | |
| 7 | | | | |
| 8 | | | | |
| 9 | | | | |
| Out | | | | |

| Hole | Yards | Par | Self | Opponent |
|------|-------|-----|------|----------|
| 10 | | | | |
| 11 | | | | |
| 12 | | | | |
| 13 | | | | |
| 14 | | | | |
| 15 | | | | |
| 16 | | | | |
| 17 | | | | |
| 18 | | | | |
| In | | | | |
| Out | | | | |
| Total | | | | |
| Handicap | | | | |
| Net Score | | | | |

Competitor's
Signature .................................................

Marker's
Signature .................................................

# Golfing Records

Course ............................................................... Date ...............................

Competition ...............................................................................

Players

| Hole | Yards | Par | Self | Opponent |
|------|-------|-----|------|----------|
| 1 | | | | |
| 2 | | | | |
| 3 | | | | |
| 4 | | | | |
| 5 | | | | |
| 6 | | | | |
| 7 | | | | |
| 8 | | | | |
| 9 | | | | |
| Out | | | | |

| Hole | Yards | Par | Self | Opponent |
|------|-------|-----|------|----------|
| 10 | | | | |
| 11 | | | | |
| 12 | | | | |
| 13 | | | | |
| 14 | | | | |
| 15 | | | | |
| 16 | | | | |
| 17 | | | | |
| 18 | | | | |
| In | | | | |
| Out | | | | |
| Total | | | | |
| Handicap | | | | |
| Net Score | | | | |

Competitor's
Signature ...............................................................

Marker's
Signature ...............................................................

## Some Men's Golf History

A form of golf was played in China 1800 years ago, while the French, Dutch and Belgians played something resembling the sport in the middle ages. However, Scotland is generally considered to be the home of golf, and the world's first golf club, the Honourable Company of Edinburgh Golfers, was founded in 1744.

The four majors in men's golf are:

British Open (first held 1860)
US Open (first held 1895)
US Masters (first held in 1934)
US PGA Championship (first held 1916)

Other important tournaments include the Ryder Cup, the World Cup and the Dunhill Cup as well as many amateur competitions.

Winner of the 1976 Dutch Open, at 19 years and 121 days, Severiano Ballesteros of Spain was the youngest winner on the European Tour. The oldest winner was Sandy Herd at 58 in 1926. The youngest winner on the American Tour was John McDermott at 19 years and 10 months in 1911, whilst the oldest was 52 year old Sam Snead in1965.

*Opposite;* **Tiger Woods**, clears a bunker in the Motorola Western Open Championship at Cog Hill 1999

# *Golfing Records*

Course ...................................................... Date ...................................

Competition ...............................................................................

Players

| Hole | Yards | Par | Self | Opponent |
|------|-------|-----|------|----------|
| 1 | | | | |
| 2 | | | | |
| 3 | | | | |
| 4 | | | | |
| 5 | | | | |
| 6 | | | | |
| 7 | | | | |
| 8 | | | | |
| 9 | | | | |
| Out | | | | |

| Hole | Yards | Par | Self | Opponent |
|------|-------|-----|------|----------|
| 10 | | | | |
| 11 | | | | |
| 12 | | | | |
| 13 | | | | |
| 14 | | | | |
| 15 | | | | |
| 16 | | | | |
| 17 | | | | |
| 18 | | | | |
| In | | | | |
| Out | | | | |
| Total | | | | |
| Handicap | | | | |
| Net Score | | | | |

Competitor's
Signature .................................................

Marker's
Signature .................................................

# *Golfing Records*

Course ...................................................................... Date ...................................

Competition ..................................................................................................

Players

| Hole | Yards | Par | Self | Opponent |
|------|-------|-----|------|----------|
| 1 | | | | |
| 2 | | | | |
| 3 | | | | |
| 4 | | | | |
| 5 | | | | |
| 6 | | | | |
| 7 | | | | |
| 8 | | | | |
| 9 | | | | |
| Out | | | | |

| Hole | Yards | Par | Self | Opponent |
|------|-------|-----|------|----------|
| 10 | | | | |
| 11 | | | | |
| 12 | | | | |
| 13 | | | | |
| 14 | | | | |
| 15 | | | | |
| 16 | | | | |
| 17 | | | | |
| 18 | | | | |
| In | | | | |
| Out | | | | |
| Total | | | | |
| Handicap | | | | |
| Net Score | | | | |

Competitor's
Signature .....................................................

Marker's
Signature .....................................................

# *Golfing Records*

Course ........................................................... Date ...................................

Competition .................................................................................................

Players

| Hole | Yards | Par | Self | Opponent |
|------|-------|-----|------|----------|
| 1 | | | | |
| 2 | | | | |
| 3 | | | | |
| 4 | | | | |
| 5 | | | | |
| 6 | | | | |
| 7 | | | | |
| 8 | | | | |
| 9 | | | | |
| Out | | | | |

| Hole | Yards | Par | Self | Opponent |
|------|-------|-----|------|----------|
| 10 | | | | |
| 11 | | | | |
| 12 | | | | |
| 13 | | | | |
| 14 | | | | |
| 15 | | | | |
| 16 | | | | |
| 17 | | | | |
| 18 | | | | |
| In | | | | |
| Out | | | | |
| Total | | | | |
| Handicap | | | | |
| Net Score | | | | |

Competitor's
Signature ..............................................................

Marker's
Signature ..............................................................

# Golfing Records

Course .................................................... Date ....................................

Competition ..........................................................................................

Players

| Hole | Yards | Par | Self | Opponent |
|------|-------|-----|------|----------|
| 1 | | | | |
| 2 | | | | |
| 3 | | | | |
| 4 | | | | |
| 5 | | | | |
| 6 | | | | |
| 7 | | | | |
| 8 | | | | |
| 9 | | | | |
| Out | | | | |

Competitor's
Signature  ....................................................

Marker's
Signature  ....................................................

| Hole | Yards | Par | Self | Opponent |
|------|-------|-----|------|----------|
| 10 | | | | |
| 11 | | | | |
| 12 | | | | |
| 13 | | | | |
| 14 | | | | |
| 15 | | | | |
| 16 | | | | |
| 17 | | | | |
| 18 | | | | |
| In | | | | |
| Out | | | | |
| Total | | | | |
| Handicap | | | | |
| Net Score | | | | |

# Golfing Records

Course ................................................................ Date ...................................

Competition ..............................................................................................

Players

| Hole | Yards | Par | Self | Opponent |
|------|-------|-----|------|----------|
| 1 | | | | |
| 2 | | | | |
| 3 | | | | |
| 4 | | | | |
| 5 | | | | |
| 6 | | | | |
| 7 | | | | |
| 8 | | | | |
| 9 | | | | |
| Out | | | | |

| Hole | Yards | Par | Self | Opponent |
|------|-------|-----|------|----------|
| 10 | | | | |
| 11 | | | | |
| 12 | | | | |
| 13 | | | | |
| 14 | | | | |
| 15 | | | | |
| 16 | | | | |
| 17 | | | | |
| 18 | | | | |
| In | | | | |
| Out | | | | |
| Total | | | | |
| Handicap | | | | |
| Net Score | | | | |

Competitor's
Signature ..................................................

Marker's
Signature ..................................................

# Golfing Records

Course ........................................................  Date ........................................

Competition ...................................................................................................

Players

| Hole | Yards | Par | Self | Opponent |
|------|-------|-----|------|----------|
| 1 | | | | |
| 2 | | | | |
| 3 | | | | |
| 4 | | | | |
| 5 | | | | |
| 6 | | | | |
| 7 | | | | |
| 8 | | | | |
| 9 | | | | |
| Out | | | | |

| Hole | Yards | Par | Self | Opponent |
|------|-------|-----|------|----------|
| 10 | | | | |
| 11 | | | | |
| 12 | | | | |
| 13 | | | | |
| 14 | | | | |
| 15 | | | | |
| 16 | | | | |
| 17 | | | | |
| 18 | | | | |
| In | | | | |
| Out | | | | |
| Total | | | | |
| Handicap | | | | |
| Net Score | | | | |

Competitor's
Signature .................................................

Marker's
Signature .................................................

| Leading Annual Money Winners Europe (1980 - 1994) | | | Leading Annual Money Winners US (1980 - 1994) | | |
|------|------|------|------|------|------|
| 1980 | Greg Norman (Aus) | £74,829 | 1980 | Tom Watson (USA) | $530,808 |
| 1981 | Bernard Langer (FRG) | £95,991 | 1981 | Tom Kite (USA) | $375,698 |
| 1982 | Sandy Lyle (UK) | £86,141 | 1982 | Craig Stadler (USA) | $446,462 |
| 1983 | Nick Faldo (UK) | £140,761 | 1983 | Hal Sutton (USA) | $426,668 |
| 1984 | Bernard Langer (FRG) | £160,883 | 1984 | Tom Watson (USA) | $476,260 |
| 1985 | Sandy Lyle (UK) | £199,020 | 1985 | Curtis Strange (USA) | $542,321 |
| 1986 | Severiano Ballesteros (Spa) | £259,275 | 1986 | Greg Norman (Aus) | $653,296 |
| 1987 | Ian Woosnam (UK) | £439,075 | 1987 | Curtis Strange (USA) | $925,941 |
| 1988 | Severiano Ballesteros (Spa) | £502,000 | 1988 | Curtis Strange (USA) | $1,147,644 |
| 1989 | Ronan Rafferty (Ire) | £465,981 | 1989 | Tom Kite (USA) | $1,395,278 |
| 1990 | Ian Woosnam (UK) | £574,166 | 1990 | Greg Norman (Aus) | $1,165,477 |
| 1991 | Severiano Ballesteros (Spa) | £545,353 | 1991 | Corey Pavin (USA) | $979,430 |
| 1992 | Nick Faldo (UK) | £708,522 | 1992 | Fred Couples (USA) | $1,344,188 |
| 1993 | Colin Montgomerie (UK) | £613,682 | 1993 | Nick Price (Zim) | $1,478,557 |
| 1994 | Colin Montgomerie (UK) | £762,719 | 1994 | Nick Price (Zim) | $1,499,927 |

*Opposite;* **Lee Trevino** USA , seen in the 1979 British Open at Royal Lytham and St. Anne's Golf Club

# Golfing Records

Course .................................................... Date ...........................

Competition ...............................................................................

Players

| Hole | Yards | Par | Self | Opponent |
|------|-------|-----|------|----------|
| 1 | | | | |
| 2 | | | | |
| 3 | | | | |
| 4 | | | | |
| 5 | | | | |
| 6 | | | | |
| 7 | | | | |
| 8 | | | | |
| 9 | | | | |
| Out | | | | |

| Hole | Yards | Par | Self | Opponent |
|------|-------|-----|------|----------|
| 10 | | | | |
| 11 | | | | |
| 12 | | | | |
| 13 | | | | |
| 14 | | | | |
| 15 | | | | |
| 16 | | | | |
| 17 | | | | |
| 18 | | | | |
| In | | | | |
| Out | | | | |
| Total | | | | |
| Handicap | | | | |
| Net Score | | | | |

Competitor's
Signature ...............................................

Marker's
Signature ...............................................

# *Golfing Records*

Course ........................................................ Date .............................

Competition .........................................................................................

Players

| Hole | Yards | Par | Self | Opponent |
|------|-------|-----|------|----------|
| 1 | | | | |
| 2 | | | | |
| 3 | | | | |
| 4 | | | | |
| 5 | | | | |
| 6 | | | | |
| 7 | | | | |
| 8 | | | | |
| 9 | | | | |
| Out | | | | |

| Hole | Yards | Par | Self | Opponent |
|------|-------|-----|------|----------|
| 10 | | | | |
| 11 | | | | |
| 12 | | | | |
| 13 | | | | |
| 14 | | | | |
| 15 | | | | |
| 16 | | | | |
| 17 | | | | |
| 18 | | | | |
| In | | | | |
| Out | | | | |
| Total | | | | |
| Handicap | | | | |
| Net Score | | | | |

Competitor's
Signature ........................................................

Marker's
Signature ........................................................

# Golfing Records

Course ...................................................... Date ..........................

Competition ..........................................................................

Players

| Hole | Yards | Par | Self | Opponent |
|------|-------|-----|------|----------|
| 1 | | | | |
| 2 | | | | |
| 3 | | | | |
| 4 | | | | |
| 5 | | | | |
| 6 | | | | |
| 7 | | | | |
| 8 | | | | |
| 9 | | | | |
| Out | | | | |

| Hole | Yards | Par | Self | Opponent |
|------|-------|-----|------|----------|
| 10 | | | | |
| 11 | | | | |
| 12 | | | | |
| 13 | | | | |
| 14 | | | | |
| 15 | | | | |
| 16 | | | | |
| 17 | | | | |
| 18 | | | | |
| In | | | | |
| Out | | | | |
| Total | | | | |
| Handicap | | | | |
| Net Score | | | | |

Competitor's
Signature ..................................................

Marker's
Signature ..................................................

# The British Open

The Open first took place at Prestwick on 17 October 1860. Eight competitors took part and the winner, Willy Park senior, won a Championship belt.

Since 1872, the Open has been played over seaside links, and the champion is awarded a silver claret jug. Today, the competition is played over 72 holes.

Prize money was introduced in 1863 and totalled £10.00. In 1995, the total had risen to £1,250,000.00.

The lowest four-round total was scored by Greg Norman in 1993 taking just 267.

At 46, Tom Morris Snr was the oldest player to win the Open (1867). Just one year after, Tom Morris Jr was the youngest to win the competition, aged 17!

## The Winners (1975-1995)

| Year | Winner | Score |
|------|--------|-------|
| 1975 | Tom Watson (USA) | 279* |
| 1976 | Johnny Miller (USA) | 279 |
| 1977 | Tom Watson (USA) | 268 |
| 1978 | Jack Nicklaus (USA) | 281 |
| 1979 | Severiano Ballesteros (Spa) | 283 |
| 1980 | Tom Watson (USA) | 271 |
| 1981 | Bill Rogers (USA) | 276 |
| 1982 | Tom Watson (USA) | 284 |
| 1983 | Tom Watson (USA) | 275 |
| 1984 | Severiano Ballesteros (Spa) | 276 |
| 1985 | Sandy Lyle (UK) | 282 |
| 1986 | Greg Norman (Aus) | 280 |
| 1987 | Nick Faldo (UK) | 279 |
| 1988 | Severiano Ballesteros (Spa) | 273 |
| 1989 | Mark Calcavecchia (USA) | 275* |
| 1990 | Nick Faldo (UK) | 270 |
| 1991 | Ian Baker-Finch (Aus) | 272 |
| 1992 | Nick Faldo (UK) | 272 |
| 1993 | Greg Norman (Aus) | 267 |
| 1994 | Nick Price (Zim) | 268 |
| 1995 | John Daly (USA) | 282* |

* After play-off

*Opposite;* **Payne Stewart**, USA seen in the USPGA Championship, Sahalee, August 1998

# Golfing Records

Course ............................................. Date ...........................

Competition ....................................................................

Players

| Hole | Yards | Par | Self | Opponent |
|------|-------|-----|------|----------|
| 1 | | | | |
| 2 | | | | |
| 3 | | | | |
| 4 | | | | |
| 5 | | | | |
| 6 | | | | |
| 7 | | | | |
| 8 | | | | |
| 9 | | | | |
| Out | | | | |

| Hole | Yards | Par | Self | Opponent |
|------|-------|-----|------|----------|
| 10 | | | | |
| 11 | | | | |
| 12 | | | | |
| 13 | | | | |
| 14 | | | | |
| 15 | | | | |
| 16 | | | | |
| 17 | | | | |
| 18 | | | | |
| In | | | | |
| Out | | | | |
| Total | | | | |
| Handicap | | | | |
| Net Score | | | | |

Competitor's
Signature ......................................

Marker's
Signature ......................................

102

A GOLF NIGHTMARE INDUCED BY THE CLUB BORE

# *Golfing Records*

Course .............................................................. Date ..............................

Competition .....................................................................................

Players

| Hole | Yards | Par | Self | Opponent |
|------|-------|-----|------|----------|
| 1 | | | | |
| 2 | | | | |
| 3 | | | | |
| 4 | | | | |
| 5 | | | | |
| 6 | | | | |
| 7 | | | | |
| 8 | | | | |
| 9 | | | | |
| Out | | | | |

| Hole | Yards | Par | Self | Opponent |
|------|-------|-----|------|----------|
| 10 | | | | |
| 11 | | | | |
| 12 | | | | |
| 13 | | | | |
| 14 | | | | |
| 15 | | | | |
| 16 | | | | |
| 17 | | | | |
| 18 | | | | |
| In | | | | |
| Out | | | | |
| Total | | | | |
| Handicap | | | | |
| Net Score | | | | |

Competitor's
Signature .............................................................

Marker's
Signature .............................................................

# *Golfing Records*

Course .................................................................... Date ...............................................

Competition ...................................................................................................................

Players

| Hole | Yards | Par | Self | Opponent |
|------|-------|-----|------|----------|
| 1 | | | | |
| 2 | | | | |
| 3 | | | | |
| 4 | | | | |
| 5 | | | | |
| 6 | | | | |
| 7 | | | | |
| 8 | | | | |
| 9 | | | | |
| Out | | | | |

| Hole | Yards | Par | Self | Opponent |
|------|-------|-----|------|----------|
| 10 | | | | |
| 11 | | | | |
| 12 | | | | |
| 13 | | | | |
| 14 | | | | |
| 15 | | | | |
| 16 | | | | |
| 17 | | | | |
| 18 | | | | |
| In | | | | |
| Out | | | | |
| Total | | | | |
| Handicap | | | | |
| Net Score | | | | |

Competitor's
Signature ...............................................................

Marker's
Signature ...............................................................

# Golfing Records

Course ........................................................  Date ...........................................

Competition ............................................................................................

Players

| Hole | Yards | Par | Self | Opponent |
|------|-------|-----|------|----------|
| 1 | | | | |
| 2 | | | | |
| 3 | | | | |
| 4 | | | | |
| 5 | | | | |
| 6 | | | | |
| 7 | | | | |
| 8 | | | | |
| 9 | | | | |
| Out | | | | |

| Hole | Yards | Par | Self | Opponent |
|------|-------|-----|------|----------|
| 10 | | | | |
| 11 | | | | |
| 12 | | | | |
| 13 | | | | |
| 14 | | | | |
| 15 | | | | |
| 16 | | | | |
| 17 | | | | |
| 18 | | | | |
| In | | | | |
| Out | | | | |
| Total | | | | |
| Handicap | | | | |
| Net Score | | | | |

Competitor's
Signature ...............................................................

Marker's
Signature ...............................................................

# Golfing Records

Course ...................................................... Date ........................................

Competition ........................................................................................

Players

| Hole | Yards | Par | Self | Opponent |
|------|-------|-----|------|----------|
| 1 | | | | |
| 2 | | | | |
| 3 | | | | |
| 4 | | | | |
| 5 | | | | |
| 6 | | | | |
| 7 | | | | |
| 8 | | | | |
| 9 | | | | |
| Out | | | | |

| Hole | Yards | Par | Self | Opponent |
|------|-------|-----|------|----------|
| 10 | | | | |
| 11 | | | | |
| 12 | | | | |
| 13 | | | | |
| 14 | | | | |
| 15 | | | | |
| 16 | | | | |
| 17 | | | | |
| 18 | | | | |
| In | | | | |
| Out | | | | |
| Total | | | | |
| Handicap | | | | |
| Net Score | | | | |

Competitor's
Signature .......................................................

Marker's
Signature .......................................................

# The US Open

The US Open was first played at Newport, Rhode Island on a 9-hole course on 4th November 1895.

The winner was English-born Horace Rawlins with a score of 173, for which he won $150.00 (the total prize money came to $335.00). In 1995, total prize money collected came to $2 million.

With the exception of the years between 1895 & 1897 the competition has been played over 72 holes.

With a score of 272 in '80, Jack Nicklaus notched up the lowest four-round total.

At 43, Raymond Floyd was the oldest player to win the US Open (1986).

In 1911, at 19, John McDermott was the youngest to win the tournament.

## The Winners (1975-1995)

| | | |
|---|---|---|
| 1975 | Lou Graham (USA) | 287 |
| 1976 | Jerry Pate (USA) | 277 |
| 1977 | Hubert Green (USA) | 278 |
| 1978 | Andy North (USA) | 285 |
| 1979 | Hale Urwin (USA) | 284 |
| 1980 | Jack Nicklaus (USA) | 272 |
| 1981 | David Graham (Aus) | 273 |
| 1982 | Tom Watson (USA) | 282 |
| 1983 | Larry Nelson (USA) | 280 |
| 1984 | Fuzzy Zoeller (USA) | 276* |
| 1985 | Andy North (USA) | 279 |
| 1986 | Raymond Floyd (USA) | 279 |
| 1987 | Scott Simpson (USA) | 277 |
| 1988 | Curtis Strange (USA) | 278 |
| 1989 | Curtis Strange (USA) | 278 |
| 1990 | Hale Urwin (USA) | 280* |
| 1991 | Payne Stewart (USA) | 282* |
| 1992 | Tom Kite (USA) | 285 |
| 1993 | Lee Janzen (USA) | 272 |
| 1994 | Ernie Els (SAf) | 279* |
| 1995 | Corey Pavin (USA) | 280 |

* After play-off

*Opposite;* **Sergio Garcia**, Spain, Volvo PGA Championship, Wentworth, 1998

# Golfing Records

Course ................................................................ Date ..............................

Competition ........................................................................................

Players

| Hole | Yards | Par | Self | Opponent |
|------|-------|-----|------|----------|
| 1 | | | | |
| 2 | | | | |
| 3 | | | | |
| 4 | | | | |
| 5 | | | | |
| 6 | | | | |
| 7 | | | | |
| 8 | | | | |
| 9 | | | | |
| Out | | | | |

| Hole | Yards | Par | Self | Opponent |
|------|-------|-----|------|----------|
| 10 | | | | |
| 11 | | | | |
| 12 | | | | |
| 13 | | | | |
| 14 | | | | |
| 15 | | | | |
| 16 | | | | |
| 17 | | | | |
| 18 | | | | |
| In | | | | |
| Out | | | | |
| Total | | | | |
| Handicap | | | | |
| Net Score | | | | |

Competitor's
Signature ...........................................................

Marker's
Signature ...........................................................

# Golfing Records

Course .......................................................... Date ........................................

Competition ..............................................................................

Players

| Hole | Yards | Par | Self | Opponent |
|------|-------|-----|------|----------|
| 1 | | | | |
| 2 | | | | |
| 3 | | | | |
| 4 | | | | |
| 5 | | | | |
| 6 | | | | |
| 7 | | | | |
| 8 | | | | |
| 9 | | | | |
| Out | | | | |

| Hole | Yards | Par | Self | Opponent |
|------|-------|-----|------|----------|
| 10 | | | | |
| 11 | | | | |
| 12 | | | | |
| 13 | | | | |
| 14 | | | | |
| 15 | | | | |
| 16 | | | | |
| 17 | | | | |
| 18 | | | | |
| In | | | | |
| Out | | | | |
| Total | | | | |
| Handicap | | | | |
| Net Score | | | | |

Competitor's
Signature ................................................

Marker's
Signature ................................................

# Golfing Records

Course ............................................................ Date ..................................

Competition ............................................................................................

Players

| Hole | Yards | Par | Self | Opponent |
|------|-------|-----|------|----------|
| 1 | | | | |
| 2 | | | | |
| 3 | | | | |
| 4 | | | | |
| 5 | | | | |
| 6 | | | | |
| 7 | | | | |
| 8 | | | | |
| 9 | | | | |
| Out | | | | |

| Hole | Yards | Par | Self | Opponent |
|------|-------|-----|------|----------|
| 10 | | | | |
| 11 | | | | |
| 12 | | | | |
| 13 | | | | |
| 14 | | | | |
| 15 | | | | |
| 16 | | | | |
| 17 | | | | |
| 18 | | | | |
| In | | | | |
| Out | | | | |
| Total | | | | |
| Handicap | | | | |
| Net Score | | | | |

Competitor's
Signature ..............................................

Marker's
Signature ..............................................

"Did you mark it, boy?"   "Ay!"
"Where is it?"   "On this yer beach!"

# *Golfing Records*

Course ............................................................  Date ............................................

Competition ................................................................................................

Players

| Hole | Yards | Par | Self | Opponent |
|------|-------|-----|------|----------|
| 1 | | | | |
| 2 | | | | |
| 3 | | | | |
| 4 | | | | |
| 5 | | | | |
| 6 | | | | |
| 7 | | | | |
| 8 | | | | |
| 9 | | | | |
| Out | | | | |

| Hole | Yards | Par | Self | Opponent |
|------|-------|-----|------|----------|
| 10 | | | | |
| 11 | | | | |
| 12 | | | | |
| 13 | | | | |
| 14 | | | | |
| 15 | | | | |
| 16 | | | | |
| 17 | | | | |
| 18 | | | | |
| In | | | | |
| Out | | | | |
| Total | | | | |
| Handicap | | | | |
| Net Score | | | | |

Competitor's
Signature ..............................................

Marker's
Signature ..............................................

# *Golfing Records*

Course ................................................................ Date ........................................

Competition ..............................................................................................

Players

| Hole | Yards | Par | Self | Opponent |
|------|-------|-----|------|----------|
| 1 | | | | |
| 2 | | | | |
| 3 | | | | |
| 4 | | | | |
| 5 | | | | |
| 6 | | | | |
| 7 | | | | |
| 8 | | | | |
| 9 | | | | |
| Out | | | | |

| Hole | Yards | Par | Self | Opponent |
|------|-------|-----|------|----------|
| 10 | | | | |
| 11 | | | | |
| 12 | | | | |
| 13 | | | | |
| 14 | | | | |
| 15 | | | | |
| 16 | | | | |
| 17 | | | | |
| 18 | | | | |
| In | | | | |
| Out | | | | |
| Total | | | | |
| Handicap | | | | |
| Net Score | | | | |

Competitor's
Signature ..................................................

Marker's
Signature ..................................................

# The US Masters

The US Masters, first introduced in 1934, was the brain child of the legendary golfer Bobby Jones, who also designed the course at Augusta, Georgia where the tournament is annually held. The first winner was Horton Smith with a score of 284.

Entry is by invitation only and the winner earns the coveted green jacket.

The competition is played over 72 holes of stroke-play.

Scoring 271 in 1965 and 1976 respectively, Jack Nicklaus and Raymond Floyd take the credit for the lowest four-round totals.

His win in 1986 made Jack Nicklaus, at 46, the oldest winner yet of the US Masters, while in 1980, Seve Ballesteros was the youngest to win – at 23.

## The Winners (1975-1995)

| Year | Winner | Score |
|------|--------|-------|
| 1975 | Jack Nicklaus (USA) | 276 |
| 1976 | Raymond Floyd (USA) | 271 |
| 1977 | Tom Watson (USA) | 276 |
| 1978 | Gary Player (SAf) | 277 |
| 1979 | Fuzzy Zoeller (USA) | 280* |
| 1980 | Severiano Ballesteros (Spa) | 275 |
| 1981 | Tom Watson (USA) | 280 |
| 1982 | Craig Stadler (USA) | 284* |
| 1983 | Severiano Ballesteros (Spa) | 280 |
| 1984 | Ben Crenshaw (USA) | 277 |
| 1985 | Bernhard Langer (FRG) | 282 |
| 1986 | Jack Nicklaus (USA) | 279 |
| 1987 | Larry Mize (USA) | 285* |
| 1988 | Sandy Lyle (UK) | 281 |
| 1989 | Nick Faldo (UK) | 283* |
| 1990 | Nick Faldo (UK) | 278* |
| 1991 | Ian Woosnam (UK) | 277 |
| 1992 | Fred Couples (USA) | 275 |
| 1993 | Bernard Langer (Ger) | 277 |
| 1994 | José Maria Olazábal (Spa) | 279 |
| 1995 | Ben Crenshaw (USA) | 274 |

* After play-off

*Opposite;* **Jack Nicklaus**, USA, action in the 1996 US Masters at Augusta National Golf Club

# Golfing Records

Course .......................................................................... Date ...................................

Competition ......................................................................................................

Players

| Hole | Yards | Par | Self | Opponent |
|------|-------|-----|------|----------|
| 1 | | | | |
| 2 | | | | |
| 3 | | | | |
| 4 | | | | |
| 5 | | | | |
| 6 | | | | |
| 7 | | | | |
| 8 | | | | |
| 9 | | | | |
| Out | | | | |

| Hole | Yards | Par | Self | Opponent |
|------|-------|-----|------|----------|
| 10 | | | | |
| 11 | | | | |
| 12 | | | | |
| 13 | | | | |
| 14 | | | | |
| 15 | | | | |
| 16 | | | | |
| 17 | | | | |
| 18 | | | | |
| In | | | | |
| Out | | | | |
| Total | | | | |
| Handicap | | | | |
| Net Score | | | | |

Competitor's
Signature ..................................................

Marker's
Signature ..................................................

# Golfing Records

Course ................................................................ Date ................................

Competition ..............................................................................................

Players

| Hole | Yards | Par | Self | Opponent |
|------|-------|-----|------|----------|
| 1 | | | | |
| 2 | | | | |
| 3 | | | | |
| 4 | | | | |
| 5 | | | | |
| 6 | | | | |
| 7 | | | | |
| 8 | | | | |
| 9 | | | | |
| Out | | | | |

Competitor's
Signature ..............................................................

Marker's
Signature ..............................................................

| Hole | Yards | Par | Self | Opponent |
|------|-------|-----|------|----------|
| 10 | | | | |
| 11 | | | | |
| 12 | | | | |
| 13 | | | | |
| 14 | | | | |
| 15 | | | | |
| 16 | | | | |
| 17 | | | | |
| 18 | | | | |
| In | | | | |
| Out | | | | |
| Total | | | | |
| Handicap | | | | |
| Net Score | | | | |

# Golfing Records

Course .................................................................... Date ........................................

Competition ...........................................................................................................

Players

| Hole | Yards | Par | Self | Opponent |
|------|-------|-----|------|----------|
| 1 | | | | |
| 2 | | | | |
| 3 | | | | |
| 4 | | | | |
| 5 | | | | |
| 6 | | | | |
| 7 | | | | |
| 8 | | | | |
| 9 | | | | |
| Out | | | | |

| Hole | Yards | Par | Self | Opponent |
|------|-------|-----|------|----------|
| 10 | | | | |
| 11 | | | | |
| 12 | | | | |
| 13 | | | | |
| 14 | | | | |
| 15 | | | | |
| 16 | | | | |
| 17 | | | | |
| 18 | | | | |
| In | | | | |
| Out | | | | |
| Total | | | | |
| Handicap | | | | |
| Net Score | | | | |

Competitor's
Signature ............................................................

Marker's
Signature ............................................................

# *Golfing Records*

Course .......................................................... Date ...............................

Competition ....................................................................................

Players

| Hole | Yards | Par | Self | Opponent |
|------|-------|-----|------|----------|
| 1 | | | | |
| 2 | | | | |
| 3 | | | | |
| 4 | | | | |
| 5 | | | | |
| 6 | | | | |
| 7 | | | | |
| 8 | | | | |
| 9 | | | | |
| Out | | | | |

| Hole | Yards | Par | Self | Opponent |
|------|-------|-----|------|----------|
| 10 | | | | |
| 11 | | | | |
| 12 | | | | |
| 13 | | | | |
| 14 | | | | |
| 15 | | | | |
| 16 | | | | |
| 17 | | | | |
| 18 | | | | |
| In | | | | |
| Out | | | | |
| Total | | | | |
| Handicap | | | | |
| Net Score | | | | |

Competitor's
Signature ........................................................

Marker's
Signature ........................................................

# Golfing Records

Course ........................................................ Date ...........................................

Competition ..............................................................................................

Players

| Hole | Yards | Par | Self | Opponent |
|------|-------|-----|------|----------|
| 1 | | | | |
| 2 | | | | |
| 3 | | | | |
| 4 | | | | |
| 5 | | | | |
| 6 | | | | |
| 7 | | | | |
| 8 | | | | |
| 9 | | | | |
| Out | | | | |

| Hole | Yards | Par | Self | Opponent |
|------|-------|-----|------|----------|
| 10 | | | | |
| 11 | | | | |
| 12 | | | | |
| 13 | | | | |
| 14 | | | | |
| 15 | | | | |
| 16 | | | | |
| 17 | | | | |
| 18 | | | | |
| In | | | | |
| Out | | | | |
| Total | | | | |
| Handicap | | | | |
| Net Score | | | | |

Competitor's
Signature ...........................................................

Marker's
Signature ...........................................................

IMPATIENT GOLFER (*to opponent, who has had shocking luck all the morning*). "Buck up, old man, I want my lunch. Where are you now?"

OPPONENT. "In a hole made by a woman's heel."

I.G. "Well, go on, knock it out! This is no time for sentiment!"

# The US PGA Championship

The US PGA Championship was first played in 1916 at Siwanoy. The winner was Jim Barnes, scoring 1 up.

It was held as a match-play event until 1958, when it became a stroke-play competition over four rounds.

Entry is based on qualification from the Professional Golfers Association tour and the competition is the least publicised of the four majors.

The lowest four-round total was scored in 1964 by Bobby Nichols, who completed in 271.

The oldest winner of the Championship was Julius Boros in 1968 at 48.

The youngest winner was Gene Sarazen in 1922 when he was just 20 years old.

## The Winners (1975-1995)

| Year | Winner | Score | | Year | Winner | Score |
|------|--------|-------|---|------|--------|-------|
| 1975 | Jack Nicklaus (USA) | 276 | | 1986 | Bob Tway (USA) | 276 |
| 1976 | Dave Stockton (USA) | 281 | | 1987 | Larry Nelson (USA) | 287* |
| 1977 | Lanny Wadkins (USA) | 282* | | 1988 | Jeff Sluman (USA) | 272 |
| 1978 | John Mahaffey (USA) | 276* | | 1989 | Payne Stewart (USA) | 276 |
| 1979 | David Graham (Aus) | 272* | | 1990 | Wayne Grady (Aus) | 282 |
| 1980 | Jack Nicklaus (USA) | 274 | | 1991 | John Daly (USA) | 276 |
| 1981 | Larry Nelson (USA) | 273 | | 1992 | Nick Price (Zim) | 278 |
| 1982 | Raymond Floyd (USA) | 272 | | 1993 | Paul Azinger (USA) | 272* |
| 1983 | Hal Sutton (USA) | 274 | | 1994 | Nick Price (Zim) | 269 |
| 1984 | Lee Trevino (USA) | 273 | | 1995 | Steve Elkington (Aus) | 267* |
| 1985 | Hubert Green (USA) | 278 | | * | After play-off | |

*Opposite;* **Tony Jacklin**, England, in the 1997 Volvo PGA Championship at Wentworth

# *Golfing Records*

Course ...................................................... Date ..........................

Competition ................................................................................

Players

| Hole | Yards | Par | Self | Opponent |
|------|-------|-----|------|----------|
| 1 | | | | |
| 2 | | | | |
| 3 | | | | |
| 4 | | | | |
| 5 | | | | |
| 6 | | | | |
| 7 | | | | |
| 8 | | | | |
| 9 | | | | |
| Out | | | | |

| Hole | Yards | Par | Self | Opponent |
|------|-------|-----|------|----------|
| 10 | | | | |
| 11 | | | | |
| 12 | | | | |
| 13 | | | | |
| 14 | | | | |
| 15 | | | | |
| 16 | | | | |
| 17 | | | | |
| 18 | | | | |
| In | | | | |
| Out | | | | |
| Total | | | | |
| Handicap | | | | |
| Net Score | | | | |

Competitor's
Signature ......................................................

Marker's
Signature ......................................................

# *Golfing Records*

Course ........................................ Date ........................................

Competition ........................................................................

Players

| Hole | Yards | Par | Self | Opponent |
|------|-------|-----|------|----------|
| 1 | | | | |
| 2 | | | | |
| 3 | | | | |
| 4 | | | | |
| 5 | | | | |
| 6 | | | | |
| 7 | | | | |
| 8 | | | | |
| 9 | | | | |
| Out | | | | |

| Hole | Yards | Par | Self | Opponent |
|------|-------|-----|------|----------|
| 10 | | | | |
| 11 | | | | |
| 12 | | | | |
| 13 | | | | |
| 14 | | | | |
| 15 | | | | |
| 16 | | | | |
| 17 | | | | |
| 18 | | | | |
| In | | | | |
| Out | | | | |
| Total | | | | |
| Handicap | | | | |
| Net Score | | | | |

Competitor's
Signature ........................................................

Marker's
Signature ........................................................

# Golfing Records

Course .......................................................... Date ...................................

Competition ...................................................................................................

Players

| Hole | Yards | Par | Self | Opponent |
|------|-------|-----|------|----------|
| 1 | | | | |
| 2 | | | | |
| 3 | | | | |
| 4 | | | | |
| 5 | | | | |
| 6 | | | | |
| 7 | | | | |
| 8 | | | | |
| 9 | | | | |
| Out | | | | |

| Hole | Yards | Par | Self | Opponent |
|------|-------|-----|------|----------|
| 10 | | | | |
| 11 | | | | |
| 12 | | | | |
| 13 | | | | |
| 14 | | | | |
| 15 | | | | |
| 16 | | | | |
| 17 | | | | |
| 18 | | | | |
| In | | | | |
| Out | | | | |
| Total | | | | |
| Handicap | | | | |
| Net Score | | | | |

Competitor's
Signature .............................................................

Marker's
Signature .............................................................

# Golfing Records

Course   ....................................................    Date   .....................................

Competition   ............................................................................................

Players

| Hole | Yards | Par | Self | Opponent |
|------|-------|-----|------|----------|
| 1 | | | | |
| 2 | | | | |
| 3 | | | | |
| 4 | | | | |
| 5 | | | | |
| 6 | | | | |
| 7 | | | | |
| 8 | | | | |
| 9 | | | | |
| Out | | | | |

| Hole | Yards | Par | Self | Opponent |
|------|-------|-----|------|----------|
| 10 | | | | |
| 11 | | | | |
| 12 | | | | |
| 13 | | | | |
| 14 | | | | |
| 15 | | | | |
| 16 | | | | |
| 17 | | | | |
| 18 | | | | |
| In | | | | |
| Out | | | | |
| Total | | | | |
| Handicap | | | | |
| Net Score | | | | |

Competitor's
Signature   .................................................

Marker's
Signature   .................................................

# Golfing Records

Course .................................................. Date ...........................

Competition ..............................................................................

Players

| Hole | Yards | Par | Self | Opponent |
|------|-------|-----|------|----------|
| 1 | | | | |
| 2 | | | | |
| 3 | | | | |
| 4 | | | | |
| 5 | | | | |
| 6 | | | | |
| 7 | | | | |
| 8 | | | | |
| 9 | | | | |
| Out | | | | |

| Hole | Yards | Par | Self | Opponent |
|------|-------|-----|------|----------|
| 10 | | | | |
| 11 | | | | |
| 12 | | | | |
| 13 | | | | |
| 14 | | | | |
| 15 | | | | |
| 16 | | | | |
| 17 | | | | |
| 18 | | | | |
| In | | | | |
| Out | | | | |
| Total | | | | |
| Handicap | | | | |
| Net Score | | | | |

Competitor's
Signature ..............................................

Marker's
Signature ..............................................

# Golfing Records

Course ...................................................... Date ...........................

Competition ...................................................................................

Players

| Hole | Yards | Par | Self | Opponent |
|------|-------|-----|------|----------|
| 1 | | | | |
| 2 | | | | |
| 3 | | | | |
| 4 | | | | |
| 5 | | | | |
| 6 | | | | |
| 7 | | | | |
| 8 | | | | |
| 9 | | | | |
| Out | | | | |

| Hole | Yards | Par | Self | Opponent |
|------|-------|-----|------|----------|
| 10 | | | | |
| 11 | | | | |
| 12 | | | | |
| 13 | | | | |
| 14 | | | | |
| 15 | | | | |
| 16 | | | | |
| 17 | | | | |
| 18 | | | | |
| In | | | | |
| Out | | | | |
| Total | | | | |
| Handicap | | | | |
| Net Score | | | | |

Competitor's
Signature ......................................................

Marker's
Signature ......................................................

# Women's Golf

The Women's Professional Golf Association (WPGA) was formed in the USA in 1944 and was reformed in 1948 as the Ladies' Professional Golf Association (LPGA).

The four majors in US women's golf are:

US Women's Open (first held 1946)

LPGA Championship (first held 1955)

Nabisco Dinah Shore (major status from 1983)

Du Maurier Classic (major status from 1979)

Mickey Wright has had the most wins since the formation of the US LPGA in 1950: she has won the US Women's Open and the LPGA Championship four times each (1958-64).

The British Women's Open Championship was first contested in 1976. It is an annual stroke-play competition.

The Women's PGA European Tour was formed in 1979.

## US LPGA
## Money Leaders (1980 - 1994)

|  |  |  |
|------|--------|----------|
| 1980 | Beth Daniel (USA) | $231,000 |
| 1981 | Beth Daniel (USA) | $206,978 |
| 1982 | JoAnne Carner (USA) | $310,399 |
| 1983 | JoAnne Carner (USA) | $291,404 |
| 1984 | Betsy King (USA) | $266,771 |
| 1985 | Nancy Lopez (USA) | $416,472 |
| 1986 | Pat Bradley (USA) | $492,021 |
| 1987 | Ayoko Okomoto (Jap) | $466,034 |
| 1988 | Sherru Turner (USA) | $350,851 |
| 1989 | Betsy King (USA) | $654,132 |
| 1990 | Beth Daniel (USA) | $863,578 |
| 1991 | Pat Bradley (USA) | $763,118 |
| 1992 | Dottie Mochrie (USA) | $693,355 |
| 1993 | Betsy King (USA) | $595,992 |
| 1994 | Laura Davies (UK) | $687,201 |

*Opposite;* **Greg Norman**, Australia, plays out of the rough in the 1993 British Open, Royal St. George's at Sandwich, Kent

# Golfing Records

Course ................................................................. Date .........................................

Competition ......................................................................................................

Players

| Hole | Yards | Par | Self | Opponent |
|------|-------|-----|------|----------|
| 1    |       |     |      |          |
| 2    |       |     |      |          |
| 3    |       |     |      |          |
| 4    |       |     |      |          |
| 5    |       |     |      |          |
| 6    |       |     |      |          |
| 7    |       |     |      |          |
| 8    |       |     |      |          |
| 9    |       |     |      |          |
| Out  |       |     |      |          |

| Hole | Yards | Par | Self | Opponent |
|------|-------|-----|------|----------|
| 10   |       |     |      |          |
| 11   |       |     |      |          |
| 12   |       |     |      |          |
| 13   |       |     |      |          |
| 14   |       |     |      |          |
| 15   |       |     |      |          |
| 16   |       |     |      |          |
| 17   |       |     |      |          |
| 18   |       |     |      |          |
| In   |       |     |      |          |
| Out  |       |     |      |          |
| Total|       |     |      |          |
| Handicap |   |     |      |          |
| Net Score |  |     |      |          |

Competitor's
Signature ...............................................................

Marker's
Signature ...............................................................

TIRESOME GOLF ENTHUSIAST. "Then observe the absorbing interest of the game: the rhythm of the swing and follow through, the nice adjustment of the approach, the careful choice of line for the putt. Each shot a problem and spur to the intellect. Small wonder that golf has so great a following. Er—what made you take it up?"

FED-UP COLONEL. "Liver."

# Golfing Records

Course .................................................... Date .......................................

Competition ...................................................................................

Players

| Hole | Yards | Par | Self | Opponent |
|------|-------|-----|------|----------|
| 1 | | | | |
| 2 | | | | |
| 3 | | | | |
| 4 | | | | |
| 5 | | | | |
| 6 | | | | |
| 7 | | | | |
| 8 | | | | |
| 9 | | | | |
| Out | | | | |

| Hole | Yards | Par | Self | Opponent |
|------|-------|-----|------|----------|
| 10 | | | | |
| 11 | | | | |
| 12 | | | | |
| 13 | | | | |
| 14 | | | | |
| 15 | | | | |
| 16 | | | | |
| 17 | | | | |
| 18 | | | | |
| In | | | | |
| Out | | | | |
| Total | | | | |
| Handicap | | | | |
| Net Score | | | | |

Competitor's
Signature ...................................................

Marker's
Signature ...................................................

# *Golfing Records*

Course .................................................... Date ...............................

Competition ......................................................................................

Players

| Hole | Yards | Par | Self | Opponent |
|------|-------|-----|------|----------|
| 1 | | | | |
| 2 | | | | |
| 3 | | | | |
| 4 | | | | |
| 5 | | | | |
| 6 | | | | |
| 7 | | | | |
| 8 | | | | |
| 9 | | | | |
| Out | | | | |

| Hole | Yards | Par | Self | Opponent |
|------|-------|-----|------|----------|
| 10 | | | | |
| 11 | | | | |
| 12 | | | | |
| 13 | | | | |
| 14 | | | | |
| 15 | | | | |
| 16 | | | | |
| 17 | | | | |
| 18 | | | | |
| In | | | | |
| Out | | | | |
| Total | | | | |
| Handicap | | | | |
| Net Score | | | | |

Competitor's
Signature .........................................................

Marker's
Signature .........................................................

# Golfing Records

Course ...................................................... Date ..................................

Competition ..........................................................................................

Players

| Hole | Yards | Par | Self | Opponent |
|------|-------|-----|------|----------|
| 1 | | | | |
| 2 | | | | |
| 3 | | | | |
| 4 | | | | |
| 5 | | | | |
| 6 | | | | |
| 7 | | | | |
| 8 | | | | |
| 9 | | | | |
| Out | | | | |

| Hole | Yards | Par | Self | Opponent |
|------|-------|-----|------|----------|
| 10 | | | | |
| 11 | | | | |
| 12 | | | | |
| 13 | | | | |
| 14 | | | | |
| 15 | | | | |
| 16 | | | | |
| 17 | | | | |
| 18 | | | | |
| In | | | | |
| Out | | | | |
| Total | | | | |
| Handicap | | | | |
| Net Score | | | | |

Competitor's
Signature  ...................................................

Marker's
Signature  ...................................................

# Golfing Records

Course ............................................................ Date ..............................

Competition ...........................................................................................

Players

| Hole | Yards | Par | Self | Opponent |
|------|-------|-----|------|----------|
| 1 | | | | |
| 2 | | | | |
| 3 | | | | |
| 4 | | | | |
| 5 | | | | |
| 6 | | | | |
| 7 | | | | |
| 8 | | | | |
| 9 | | | | |
| Out | | | | |

| Hole | Yards | Par | Self | Opponent |
|------|-------|-----|------|----------|
| 10 | | | | |
| 11 | | | | |
| 12 | | | | |
| 13 | | | | |
| 14 | | | | |
| 15 | | | | |
| 16 | | | | |
| 17 | | | | |
| 18 | | | | |
| In | | | | |
| Out | | | | |
| Total | | | | |
| Handicap | | | | |
| Net Score | | | | |

Competitor's
Signature .............................................................

Marker's
Signature .............................................................

## Womens' PGA European Tour Money Leaders (1980 - 1994)

|  |  |  |
|------|--------|----------|
| 1980 | Muriel Thomson (UK) | £8,008 |
| 1981 | Jenny Lee Smith (UK) | £13,519 |
| 1982 | Jenny Lee Smith (UK) | £12,551 |
| 1983 | Beverly Huke (UK) | £9,226 |
| 1984 | Dale Reid (UK) | £28,239 |
| 1985 | Laura Davies (UK) | £21,736 |
| 1986 | Laura Davies (UK) | £37,500 |
| 1987 | Dale Reid (UK) | £53,815 |
| 1988 | Marie-Laure de Lorenzi (Fra) | £99,360 |
| 1989 | Marie-Laure de Lorenzi (Fra) | £77,534 |
| 1990 | Trish Johnson (UK) | £83,403 |
| 1991 | Corinne Dibnah (Aus) | £89,058 |
| 1992 | Laura Davies (UK) | £66,333 |
| 1993 | Karen Lunn (Aus) | £66,266 |
| 1994 | Liselotte Neumann (Swe) | £102,750 |

*Opposite;* **Arnold Palmer**, USA, in the 1994 US Masters, at Augusta

# Golfing Records

Course ............................................................. Date ...........................

Competition ....................................................................................

Players

| Hole | Yards | Par | Self | Opponent |
|------|-------|-----|------|----------|
| 1 | | | | |
| 2 | | | | |
| 3 | | | | |
| 4 | | | | |
| 5 | | | | |
| 6 | | | | |
| 7 | | | | |
| 8 | | | | |
| 9 | | | | |
| Out | | | | |

| Hole | Yards | Par | Self | Opponent |
|------|-------|-----|------|----------|
| 10 | | | | |
| 11 | | | | |
| 12 | | | | |
| 13 | | | | |
| 14 | | | | |
| 15 | | | | |
| 16 | | | | |
| 17 | | | | |
| 18 | | | | |
| In | | | | |
| Out | | | | |
| Total | | | | |
| Handicap | | | | |
| Net Score | | | | |

Competitor's
Signature .................................................

Marker's
Signature .................................................

# *Golfing Records*

Course ...................................................................... Date ..................................

Competition ...............................................................................................

Players

| Hole | Yards | Par | Self | Opponent |
|------|-------|-----|------|----------|
| 1 | | | | |
| 2 | | | | |
| 3 | | | | |
| 4 | | | | |
| 5 | | | | |
| 6 | | | | |
| 7 | | | | |
| 8 | | | | |
| 9 | | | | |
| Out | | | | |

Competitor's
Signature ...............................................................

Marker's
Signature ...............................................................

| Hole | Yards | Par | Self | Opponent |
|------|-------|-----|------|----------|
| 10 | | | | |
| 11 | | | | |
| 12 | | | | |
| 13 | | | | |
| 14 | | | | |
| 15 | | | | |
| 16 | | | | |
| 17 | | | | |
| 18 | | | | |
| In | | | | |
| Out | | | | |
| Total | | | | |
| Handicap | | | | |
| Net Score | | | | |

# Golfing Records

Course .................................................... Date ...................................

Competition ..........................................................................................

Players

| Hole | Yards | Par | Self | Opponent |
|------|-------|-----|------|----------|
| 1 | | | | |
| 2 | | | | |
| 3 | | | | |
| 4 | | | | |
| 5 | | | | |
| 6 | | | | |
| 7 | | | | |
| 8 | | | | |
| 9 | | | | |
| Out | | | | |

| Hole | Yards | Par | Self | Opponent |
|------|-------|-----|------|----------|
| 10 | | | | |
| 11 | | | | |
| 12 | | | | |
| 13 | | | | |
| 14 | | | | |
| 15 | | | | |
| 16 | | | | |
| 17 | | | | |
| 18 | | | | |
| In | | | | |
| Out | | | | |
| Total | | | | |
| Handicap | | | | |
| Net Score | | | | |

Competitor's
Signature ....................................................

Marker's
Signature ....................................................

HEART-BROKEN COMPETITOR (*who has missed a quick putt*). "Now wouldn't you call that provoking?"

CADDIE. "Well, Miss, that's a word I don't use meself."

# *Golfing Records*

Course .................................................. Date ........................................

Competition ..................................................................................

Players

| Hole | Yards | Par | Self | Opponent |
|------|-------|-----|------|----------|
| 1 | | | | |
| 2 | | | | |
| 3 | | | | |
| 4 | | | | |
| 5 | | | | |
| 6 | | | | |
| 7 | | | | |
| 8 | | | | |
| 9 | | | | |
| Out | | | | |

| Hole | Yards | Par | Self | Opponent |
|------|-------|-----|------|----------|
| 10 | | | | |
| 11 | | | | |
| 12 | | | | |
| 13 | | | | |
| 14 | | | | |
| 15 | | | | |
| 16 | | | | |
| 17 | | | | |
| 18 | | | | |
| In | | | | |
| Out | | | | |
| Total | | | | |
| Handicap | | | | |
| Net Score | | | | |

Competitor's
Signature .....................................................

Marker's
Signature .....................................................

# *Golfing Records*

Course .................................................................... Date ........................................

Competition ....................................................................................................

Players

| Hole | Yards | Par | Self | Opponent |
|------|-------|-----|------|----------|
| 1 | | | | |
| 2 | | | | |
| 3 | | | | |
| 4 | | | | |
| 5 | | | | |
| 6 | | | | |
| 7 | | | | |
| 8 | | | | |
| 9 | | | | |
| Out | | | | |

| Hole | Yards | Par | Self | Opponent |
|------|-------|-----|------|----------|
| 10 | | | | |
| 11 | | | | |
| 12 | | | | |
| 13 | | | | |
| 14 | | | | |
| 15 | | | | |
| 16 | | | | |
| 17 | | | | |
| 18 | | | | |
| In | | | | |
| Out | | | | |
| Total | | | | |
| Handicap | | | | |
| Net Score | | | | |

Competitor's
Signature ...............................................................

Marker's
Signature ...............................................................

*Opposite*; **Tom Watson**, USA, with the Claret Jug Trophy from the 1983 British Open at Royal Birkdale

# Golfing Records

Course ............................................................ Date ...................................

Competition ............................................................................................

Players

| Hole | Yards | Par | Self | Opponent |
|------|-------|-----|------|----------|
| 1 | | | | |
| 2 | | | | |
| 3 | | | | |
| 4 | | | | |
| 5 | | | | |
| 6 | | | | |
| 7 | | | | |
| 8 | | | | |
| 9 | | | | |
| Out | | | | |

| Hole | Yards | Par | Self | Opponent |
|------|-------|-----|------|----------|
| 10 | | | | |
| 11 | | | | |
| 12 | | | | |
| 13 | | | | |
| 14 | | | | |
| 15 | | | | |
| 16 | | | | |
| 17 | | | | |
| 18 | | | | |
| In | | | | |
| Out | | | | |
| Total | | | | |
| Handicap | | | | |
| Net Score | | | | |

Competitor's
Signature ............................................................

Marker's
Signature ............................................................

# Golfing Records

Course ........................................................ Date ........................................

Competition ....................................................................................

Players

| Hole | Yards | Par | Self | Opponent |
|------|-------|-----|------|----------|
| 1 | | | | |
| 2 | | | | |
| 3 | | | | |
| 4 | | | | |
| 5 | | | | |
| 6 | | | | |
| 7 | | | | |
| 8 | | | | |
| 9 | | | | |
| Out | | | | |

| Hole | Yards | Par | Self | Opponent |
|------|-------|-----|------|----------|
| 10 | | | | |
| 11 | | | | |
| 12 | | | | |
| 13 | | | | |
| 14 | | | | |
| 15 | | | | |
| 16 | | | | |
| 17 | | | | |
| 18 | | | | |
| In | | | | |
| Out | | | | |
| Total | | | | |
| Handicap | | | | |
| Net Score | | | | |

Competitor's
Signature ....................................................

Marker's
Signature ....................................................

# Golfing Records

Course ........................................................................ Date .............................................

Competition ..............................................................................................................

Players

| Hole | Yards | Par | Self | Opponent |
|------|-------|-----|------|----------|
| 1 | | | | |
| 2 | | | | |
| 3 | | | | |
| 4 | | | | |
| 5 | | | | |
| 6 | | | | |
| 7 | | | | |
| 8 | | | | |
| 9 | | | | |
| Out | | | | |

| Hole | Yards | Par | Self | Opponent |
|------|-------|-----|------|----------|
| 10 | | | | |
| 11 | | | | |
| 12 | | | | |
| 13 | | | | |
| 14 | | | | |
| 15 | | | | |
| 16 | | | | |
| 17 | | | | |
| 18 | | | | |
| In | | | | |
| Out | | | | |
| Total | | | | |
| Handicap | | | | |
| Net Score | | | | |

Competitor's
Signature ...............................................................

Marker's
Signature ...............................................................

# *Golfing Records*

Course ........................................................... Date ...............................

Competition ...............................................................................................

Players

| Hole | Yards | Par | Self | Opponent |
|------|-------|-----|------|----------|
| 1 | | | | |
| 2 | | | | |
| 3 | | | | |
| 4 | | | | |
| 5 | | | | |
| 6 | | | | |
| 7 | | | | |
| 8 | | | | |
| 9 | | | | |
| Out | | | | |

| Hole | Yards | Par | Self | Opponent |
|------|-------|-----|------|----------|
| 10 | | | | |
| 11 | | | | |
| 12 | | | | |
| 13 | | | | |
| 14 | | | | |
| 15 | | | | |
| 16 | | | | |
| 17 | | | | |
| 18 | | | | |
| In | | | | |
| Out | | | | |
| Total | | | | |
| Handicap | | | | |
| Net Score | | | | |

Competitor's
Signature .............................................................

Marker's
Signature .............................................................

# Golfing Records

Course ......................................................... Date ..........................

Competition ...........................................................................

Players

| Hole | Yards | Par | Self | Opponent |
|------|-------|-----|------|----------|
| 1 | | | | |
| 2 | | | | |
| 3 | | | | |
| 4 | | | | |
| 5 | | | | |
| 6 | | | | |
| 7 | | | | |
| 8 | | | | |
| 9 | | | | |
| Out | | | | |

Competitor's
Signature ...........................................................

Marker's
Signature ...........................................................

| Hole | Yards | Par | Self | Opponent |
|------|-------|-----|------|----------|
| 10 | | | | |
| 11 | | | | |
| 12 | | | | |
| 13 | | | | |
| 14 | | | | |
| 15 | | | | |
| 16 | | | | |
| 17 | | | | |
| 18 | | | | |
| In | | | | |
| Out | | | | |
| Total | | | | |
| Handicap | | | | |
| Net Score | | | | |

"My dear Sir, if you heard me shout 'Fore' why the deuce didn't you do it?"

*Opposite;* **Nick Faldo,** from the 1996 US Masters at Augusta National Golf Club

# Golfing Records

Course ............................................................ Date ...................................

Competition ...............................................................................................

Players

| Hole | Yards | Par | Self | Opponent |
|------|-------|-----|------|----------|
| 1 | | | | |
| 2 | | | | |
| 3 | | | | |
| 4 | | | | |
| 5 | | | | |
| 6 | | | | |
| 7 | | | | |
| 8 | | | | |
| 9 | | | | |
| Out | | | | |

| Hole | Yards | Par | Self | Opponent |
|------|-------|-----|------|----------|
| 10 | | | | |
| 11 | | | | |
| 12 | | | | |
| 13 | | | | |
| 14 | | | | |
| 15 | | | | |
| 16 | | | | |
| 17 | | | | |
| 18 | | | | |
| In | | | | |
| Out | | | | |
| Total | | | | |
| Handicap | | | | |
| Net Score | | | | |

Competitor's
Signature ...............................................................

Marker's
Signature ...............................................................

# *Golfing Records*

Course .................................................. Date ....................................

Competition ...............................................................................

Players

| Hole | Yards | Par | Self | Opponent |
|------|-------|-----|------|----------|
| 1 | | | | |
| 2 | | | | |
| 3 | | | | |
| 4 | | | | |
| 5 | | | | |
| 6 | | | | |
| 7 | | | | |
| 8 | | | | |
| 9 | | | | |
| Out | | | | |

| Hole | Yards | Par | Self | Opponent |
|------|-------|-----|------|----------|
| 10 | | | | |
| 11 | | | | |
| 12 | | | | |
| 13 | | | | |
| 14 | | | | |
| 15 | | | | |
| 16 | | | | |
| 17 | | | | |
| 18 | | | | |
| In | | | | |
| Out | | | | |
| Total | | | | |
| Handicap | | | | |
| Net Score | | | | |

Competitor's
Signature ..................................................

Marker's
Signature ..................................................

# Golfing Records

Course  .................................................. Date  ..............................

Competition ..................................................................

Players

| Hole | Yards | Par | Self | Opponent |
|------|-------|-----|------|----------|
| 1 | | | | |
| 2 | | | | |
| 3 | | | | |
| 4 | | | | |
| 5 | | | | |
| 6 | | | | |
| 7 | | | | |
| 8 | | | | |
| 9 | | | | |
| Out | | | | |

| Hole | Yards | Par | Self | Opponent |
|------|-------|-----|------|----------|
| 10 | | | | |
| 11 | | | | |
| 12 | | | | |
| 13 | | | | |
| 14 | | | | |
| 15 | | | | |
| 16 | | | | |
| 17 | | | | |
| 18 | | | | |
| In | | | | |
| Out | | | | |
| Total | | | | |
| Handicap | | | | |
| Net Score | | | | |

Competitor's
Signature  ............................................

Marker's
Signature  ............................................

# *Golfing Records*

Course .......................................................... Date ...................................

Competition ...............................................................................................

Players

| Hole | Yards | Par | Self | Opponent |
|------|-------|-----|------|----------|
| 1 | | | | |
| 2 | | | | |
| 3 | | | | |
| 4 | | | | |
| 5 | | | | |
| 6 | | | | |
| 7 | | | | |
| 8 | | | | |
| 9 | | | | |
| Out | | | | |

| Hole | Yards | Par | Self | Opponent |
|------|-------|-----|------|----------|
| 10 | | | | |
| 11 | | | | |
| 12 | | | | |
| 13 | | | | |
| 14 | | | | |
| 15 | | | | |
| 16 | | | | |
| 17 | | | | |
| 18 | | | | |
| In | | | | |
| Out | | | | |
| Total | | | | |
| Handicap | | | | |
| Net Score | | | | |

Competitor's
Signature .................................................

Marker's
Signature .................................................

# Golfing Records

Course .................................................... Date ...........................

Competition ..............................................................................

Players

| Hole | Yards | Par | Self | Opponent |
|------|-------|-----|------|----------|
| 1 | | | | |
| 2 | | | | |
| 3 | | | | |
| 4 | | | | |
| 5 | | | | |
| 6 | | | | |
| 7 | | | | |
| 8 | | | | |
| 9 | | | | |
| Out | | | | |

| Hole | Yards | Par | Self | Opponent |
|------|-------|-----|------|----------|
| 10 | | | | |
| 11 | | | | |
| 12 | | | | |
| 13 | | | | |
| 14 | | | | |
| 15 | | | | |
| 16 | | | | |
| 17 | | | | |
| 18 | | | | |
| In | | | | |
| Out | | | | |
| Total | | | | |
| Handicap | | | | |
| Net Score | | | | |

Competitor's
Signature ................................................

Marker's
Signature ................................................

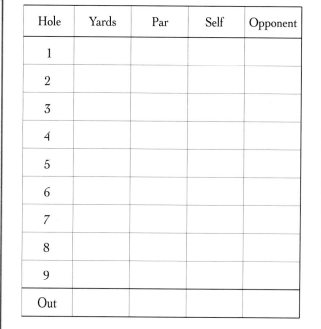

162

# Golfing Records

Course ...................................................... Date ...........................................

Competition ...............................................................................................

Players

| Hole | Yards | Par | Self | Opponent |
|------|-------|-----|------|----------|
| 1 | | | | |
| 2 | | | | |
| 3 | | | | |
| 4 | | | | |
| 5 | | | | |
| 6 | | | | |
| 7 | | | | |
| 8 | | | | |
| 9 | | | | |
| Out | | | | |

| Hole | Yards | Par | Self | Opponent |
|------|-------|-----|------|----------|
| 10 | | | | |
| 11 | | | | |
| 12 | | | | |
| 13 | | | | |
| 14 | | | | |
| 15 | | | | |
| 16 | | | | |
| 17 | | | | |
| 18 | | | | |
| In | | | | |
| Out | | | | |
| Total | | | | |
| Handicap | | | | |
| Net Score | | | | |

Competitor's
Signature ......................................................

Marker's
Signature ......................................................

*Opposite;* **Seve Ballesteros**, hitting hard in the 1988 British Open at
Royal Lytham St. Anne's

# Golfing Records

Course .................................................. Date ...........................

Competition ...................................................................................

Players

| Hole | Yards | Par | Self | Opponent |
|------|-------|-----|------|----------|
| 1 | | | | |
| 2 | | | | |
| 3 | | | | |
| 4 | | | | |
| 5 | | | | |
| 6 | | | | |
| 7 | | | | |
| 8 | | | | |
| 9 | | | | |
| Out | | | | |

| Hole | Yards | Par | Self | Opponent |
|------|-------|-----|------|----------|
| 10 | | | | |
| 11 | | | | |
| 12 | | | | |
| 13 | | | | |
| 14 | | | | |
| 15 | | | | |
| 16 | | | | |
| 17 | | | | |
| 18 | | | | |
| In | | | | |
| Out | | | | |
| Total | | | | |
| Handicap | | | | |
| Net Score | | | | |

Competitor's
Signature ...........................................

Marker's
Signature ...........................................

VERY MINIATURE GOLF: AN AFTER-DINNER ROUND

# Golfing Records

Course .................................................... Date ...................................

Competition ....................................................................................

Players

| Hole | Yards | Par | Self | Opponent |
|------|-------|-----|------|----------|
| 1 | | | | |
| 2 | | | | |
| 3 | | | | |
| 4 | | | | |
| 5 | | | | |
| 6 | | | | |
| 7 | | | | |
| 8 | | | | |
| 9 | | | | |
| Out | | | | |

| Hole | Yards | Par | Self | Opponent |
|------|-------|-----|------|----------|
| 10 | | | | |
| 11 | | | | |
| 12 | | | | |
| 13 | | | | |
| 14 | | | | |
| 15 | | | | |
| 16 | | | | |
| 17 | | | | |
| 18 | | | | |
| In | | | | |
| Out | | | | |
| Total | | | | |
| Handicap | | | | |
| Net Score | | | | |

Competitor's
Signature ...................................................

Marker's
Signature ...................................................

# Golfing Records

Course ............................................................................ Date ..............................................

Competition ....................................................................................................................

Players

| Hole | Yards | Par | Self | Opponent |
|------|-------|-----|------|----------|
| 1 | | | | |
| 2 | | | | |
| 3 | | | | |
| 4 | | | | |
| 5 | | | | |
| 6 | | | | |
| 7 | | | | |
| 8 | | | | |
| 9 | | | | |
| Out | | | | |

| Hole | Yards | Par | Self | Opponent |
|------|-------|-----|------|----------|
| 10 | | | | |
| 11 | | | | |
| 12 | | | | |
| 13 | | | | |
| 14 | | | | |
| 15 | | | | |
| 16 | | | | |
| 17 | | | | |
| 18 | | | | |
| In | | | | |
| Out | | | | |
| Total | | | | |
| Handicap | | | | |
| Net Score | | | | |

Competitor's
Signature ......................................................................

Marker's
Signature ......................................................................

# Golfing Records

Course .............................................................. Date ...............................

Competition ...................................................................................

Players

| Hole | Yards | Par | Self | Opponent |
|------|-------|-----|------|----------|
| 1 | | | | |
| 2 | | | | |
| 3 | | | | |
| 4 | | | | |
| 5 | | | | |
| 6 | | | | |
| 7 | | | | |
| 8 | | | | |
| 9 | | | | |
| Out | | | | |

| Hole | Yards | Par | Self | Opponent |
|------|-------|-----|------|----------|
| 10 | | | | |
| 11 | | | | |
| 12 | | | | |
| 13 | | | | |
| 14 | | | | |
| 15 | | | | |
| 16 | | | | |
| 17 | | | | |
| 18 | | | | |
| In | | | | |
| Out | | | | |
| Total | | | | |
| Handicap | | | | |
| Net Score | | | | |

Competitor's
Signature .................................................

Marker's
Signature .................................................

# Golfing Records

Course ............................................................ Date ..................................

Competition ........................................................................................

Players

| Hole | Yards | Par | Self | Opponent |
|------|-------|-----|------|----------|
| 1 | | | | |
| 2 | | | | |
| 3 | | | | |
| 4 | | | | |
| 5 | | | | |
| 6 | | | | |
| 7 | | | | |
| 8 | | | | |
| 9 | | | | |
| Out | | | | |

| Hole | Yards | Par | Self | Opponent |
|------|-------|-----|------|----------|
| 10 | | | | |
| 11 | | | | |
| 12 | | | | |
| 13 | | | | |
| 14 | | | | |
| 15 | | | | |
| 16 | | | | |
| 17 | | | | |
| 18 | | | | |
| In | | | | |
| Out | | | | |
| Total | | | | |
| Handicap | | | | |
| Net Score | | | | |

Competitor's
Signature ...............................................................

Marker's
Signature ...............................................................

*Opposite;* **Bernhard Langer**, Germany, in the 1992 US Masters at Augusta

# Golfing Records

Course ........................................................ Date ...................................

Competition ........................................................................................

Players

| Hole | Yards | Par | Self | Opponent |
|------|-------|-----|------|----------|
| 1 | | | | |
| 2 | | | | |
| 3 | | | | |
| 4 | | | | |
| 5 | | | | |
| 6 | | | | |
| 7 | | | | |
| 8 | | | | |
| 9 | | | | |
| Out | | | | |

| Hole | Yards | Par | Self | Opponent |
|------|-------|-----|------|----------|
| 10 | | | | |
| 11 | | | | |
| 12 | | | | |
| 13 | | | | |
| 14 | | | | |
| 15 | | | | |
| 16 | | | | |
| 17 | | | | |
| 18 | | | | |
| In | | | | |
| Out | | | | |
| Total | | | | |
| Handicap | | | | |
| Net Score | | | | |

Competitor's
Signature ...................................................

Marker's
Signature ...................................................

# *Golfing Records*

Course ...................................................... Date ........................................

Competition ..................................................................................................

Players

| Hole | Yards | Par | Self | Opponent |
|------|-------|-----|------|----------|
| 1 | | | | |
| 2 | | | | |
| 3 | | | | |
| 4 | | | | |
| 5 | | | | |
| 6 | | | | |
| 7 | | | | |
| 8 | | | | |
| 9 | | | | |
| Out | | | | |

| Hole | Yards | Par | Self | Opponent |
|------|-------|-----|------|----------|
| 10 | | | | |
| 11 | | | | |
| 12 | | | | |
| 13 | | | | |
| 14 | | | | |
| 15 | | | | |
| 16 | | | | |
| 17 | | | | |
| 18 | | | | |
| In | | | | |
| Out | | | | |
| Total | | | | |
| Handicap | | | | |
| Net Score | | | | |

Competitor's
Signature ..................................................

Marker's
Signature ..................................................

175

# Golfing Records

Course ..................................................... Date ...................................

Competition ...........................................................................................

Players

| Hole | Yards | Par | Self | Opponent |
|------|-------|-----|------|----------|
| 1 | | | | |
| 2 | | | | |
| 3 | | | | |
| 4 | | | | |
| 5 | | | | |
| 6 | | | | |
| 7 | | | | |
| 8 | | | | |
| 9 | | | | |
| Out | | | | |

| Hole | Yards | Par | Self | Opponent |
|------|-------|-----|------|----------|
| 10 | | | | |
| 11 | | | | |
| 12 | | | | |
| 13 | | | | |
| 14 | | | | |
| 15 | | | | |
| 16 | | | | |
| 17 | | | | |
| 18 | | | | |
| In | | | | |
| Out | | | | |
| Total | | | | |
| Handicap | | | | |
| Net Score | | | | |

Competitor's
Signature ...........................................................

Marker's
Signature ...........................................................

THE TIGRESS. "Let's see—what's your handicap?"
THE RABBIT. "Twenty-four; but I'm fairly bright otherwise."

RETIRED M.F.H. "And when we came to the seventeenth, just as I was going to drive, what should I see but an old dog fox staring at me out of the hedge!"

SYMPATHETIC FRIEND. "Ye-e-e-s?"

RETIRED M.F.H. "Now, don't you think that was a most remarkable thing?"

SYMPATHETIC FRIEND. "Well, yes, I suppose it was; but then, you see, I don't know anything about golf."

# The Fun
## of
# Golf

The entire handbook can be reduced to three rules. One: you do not touch your ball from the time you tee it up to the moment you pick it out of the hole. Two: don't bend over when you are in the rough. Three: when you are in the woods, keep clapping your hands.

*Charles Price*

## THE GOLF STREAM

Flows along the Eastern Coast of Scotland during the Summer and Autumn.

10 A.M.

Golf is a game whose aim is to hit a very small ball into an even smaller hole, with weapons singularly ill-designed for the purpose.

*Sir Winston Churchill*

## THE ARROGANCE OF WEALTH

*Lady Golfer (With great Assurance).* "MINE'S THE TWO-SHILLING BALL".

Golf is not like tennis, or basketball, or football, where you can control your opponent. With golf you cannot control your opponent.

*Tom Kite*

Caddies are a breed of their own. If you shoot a 66, they'll say, 'Man, we shot a 66!' But go and shoot 77 and they'll say, 'Hell, he shot a 77!'

*Lee Trevino*

## ENCOURAGEMENT.

*Professional golfer (in answer to anxious question).* "WEELL, NO SIR, AT YOUR TIME 'O LIFE,
YE CAN NEVER HOPE TO BECOME A *PLAYER*; BUT IF YE PRACTISE HARD FOR THREE YEARS, YE
MAY BE ABLE TO TELL GOOD PLAY FROM BAD WHEN YE SEE IT!'.

True golfers do not play the game as a form of stress management. Quite the reverse. They play to establish superiority over (*a*) themselves, (*b*) inanimate objects such as a small white ball with dimples in it, and (*c*) their friends. All of which can become rather tedious.

*Colin Bowles*

## VERY ADVANCED GOLF.

I. This for it!    II. Holed!

Golf is like a love affair. If you don't take it seriously, it's no fun; if you do take it seriously, it breaks your heart.

*Arnold Daly*

SCENE-*A London omnibus. Two ladies of somewhat mature age discussing their respective golf handicaps.*

*First Lady.* "WHAT ARE YOU?"

*Second Lady.* "OH I'VE BEEN SEVENTEEN ALL ALONG!"

*Elderly Party (rather merry, who has been listening).* "HO YUSS, AN I'VE STUCK AT NINETEEN!"

10·12

I still swing the way I used to, but when I look up the ball is going in a different direction.

*Lee Trevino*

!!!!!

*Lily* (*from Devonshire, on a visit to her Scotch cousin Margy in St. Andrews, N.B.*)
"WHAT A STRANGE THING FASHION IS, MARGY! FANCY A GAME LIKE GOLF REACHING UP
AS FAR NORTH AS THIS!"

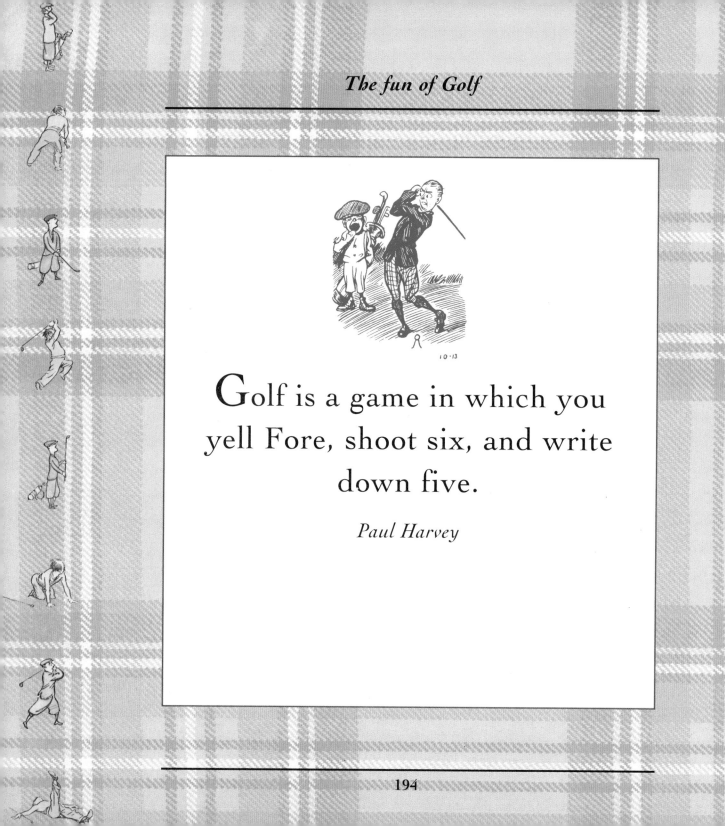

Golf is a game in which you yell Fore, shoot six, and write down five.

*Paul Harvey*

## A LAST RESORT.

*Miss Armstrong (who has foozled the ball six times with various clubs)* "AND WHICH OF THE STICKS AM I TO USE NOW?"

*Weary Caddie.* "GIE IT A BIT KNOCK WI' THE BAG!"

I call my putter *'Sweet Charity'* because it covers such a multitude of sins from tee to green.

*Billy Casper*

## THE RETORT COURTEOUS.

*The Major General (waiting to drive, to girl carrying baby, who blocks the way.)*

"Now then, hurry on please with that baby."

Girl. "Garn! Baby yerself playing at ball there in your knickerbockers an' all.

$A$t least he can't cheat on his score – because all you have to do is look back down the fairway and count the wounded.

*Bob Hope*

*Caddie (in stage whisper to Biffin, who is frightfully nervous).* "DON'T YOU GET NERVOUS , SIR! IT'S ALL RIGHT. I'VE TOLD EVERY ONE OF 'EM YOU CAN'T PLAY!"

$A$ctually, the only time I ever took out a one-iron was to kill a tarantula. And I took a seven to do that.

*Jim Murray*

JONES HAS RECENTLY TAKEN UP GOLF. HE IS ALREADY PROFICIENT IN ONE DEPARTMENT—
THE ART OF ADDRESSING THE BALL.

${\rm T}$here is one essential only in
the golf swing, the ball
must be hit.

*Sir Walter Simpson*

## AN EXCUSABLE MISTAKE.

*Miggs and Griggs who have got away for a week-end holiday, have strayed on to the Golf Links,*
*and have been watching the Colonel, who has been bunkered for the last ten minutes.*

*Miggs.* "What's he doing?"

*Griggs.* "I dunno. Think he's trying to kill something."

I don't like doctors. They are like golfers. Every one has a different answer to your problem.

*Severiano Ballesteros*

## UNFEELING.

*Voice from over the Hedge.* "OH DO MAKE HASTE GEORGE! YOU ARE A TIME!"

## DISTINCTION WITHOUT DIFFERENCE.

*Sensitive Golfer who has foozled.* "DID YOU LAUGH AT ME BOY?"

*Caddie.* "NO SIR I WAS LAUGHIN' AT ANOTHER MAN."

*Sensitive Golfer.* "AND WHAT'S FUNNY ABOUT HIM?"

*Caddie.* "HE PLAYS GOWF AWFU' LIKE YOU, SIR!"

10·27

Ah well. If we hit it perfect every day, everybody else would quit.

*Lee Trevino to Tom Watson*

Cheerful beginner (*who has just smashed the Colonel's favourite driver*). "Oh, NOW I SEE WHY YOU HAVE TO CARRY SO MANY CLUBS".

Players should pick up bomb
and shell splinters from the
fairways in order to save
damage to the mowers.

*British War Rule*

*First Golfer* (*to second golfer who is caught in a bunker*). "WELL JONES TOLD ME THIS
MORNING HE DID THIS HOLE YESTERDAY IN FOUR."

*Second golfer* (*who stammers*) " IF JONES SAID HE DID IT IN FOUR HE WAS A L-L-L-"

*First Golfer.* "STEADY FRIEND, STEADY!" SECOND GOLFER. "HE WAS A L-L-LUCKY BEGGAR!"

I've noticed some of them are
off balance when they swing.
They're top-heavy. They've got
too much hair.

*Ben Hogan on today's golfers (1970)*

THE ENGLISH WIFE.

THE AMERICAN HUSBAND.

# When they start hitting back at me, it's time to quit.

*Henry Ransom (when a shot rebounded from a cliff and hit him in the stomach)*

## THE MISERIES OF A *VERY* AMATEUR GOLFER.

He is very shy and unfortunately has to drive off in front of the Lady
Champion and a large gallery. He makes a tremendous effort. The ball
travels at least Five Yards!

The amateur who picks up his newspaper and remarks that he could shoot better golf than those guys on tour should pause and consider the prospects very carefully . . . It is not just a different game.
It is not a game at all.

*Peter Dobereiner*

## A THRIFTY MIND.

*Faithful wife (unable to restrain her feelings).*
"FRANKIE DEAR, SURELY IT'S NOT WORTH
SPOILING YOUR NEW SUIT!"

## ERRATIC.

*Pedestrian (anxious for his safety).*
"NOW WHICH WAY ARE YOU GOING
TO HIT THE BALL?"
*Worried Beginner.* "ONLY WISH TO
GOODNESS I KNEW MYSELF!"

Confidence builds with successive putts. The putter, then, is a club designed to hit the ball partway to the hole.

*Rex Lardner*

## THE HILLSIDE TEE.

COLONEL CHUTNEIGH. "SEEMS TO ME (*pouf*) THIS WHATYERMAYCALLIT WHERE YOU DRIVE
OFF IS THE ONLY DECENT THING THE COMMITTEE'S DONE ON THE WHOLE LINKS.
DEUCED CONVENIENT FOR TEEING UP YOUR BALL.
WHY THE DICKENS CAN'T THEY MAKE 'EM ALL LIKE IT?"

Golf is a fickle game, and must be wooed to be won.

*Willy Park Jr*

GOLF A LA WATTEAU-AND OTHERWISE.

$I$t's funny, but the more I
practice, the
luckier I become.

*Gary Player*

## AND YET THEY EXPECT THE VOTE

*Caddy.* "Say, Miss we're just going to drive off on to that green."

*Aunty.* "Oh thank the gentleman so much for sending you to tell us. Then we shall have a beautiful view.

If you try to break the ball to pieces, the sod may fly farther than your shots. You've got to be gentle. Sweet-talk that ball. Make it your friend and it will stay with you a lot longer.

*Sam Snead*

*Golfer (soliloquising).* "What a lovely view!"

*Caddie.* "Reg'lar panama I calls it!"

The difference between learning to play golf and learning to drive a car is that in golf you never hit anything.

*Anon*

*Little Albert (always thirsting for knowledge).* "UNCLE, DO THEY PRONOUNCE THAT *ricochaying* OR *ricochetting?*"

**I**f you watch a game, it's fun. If you play it, it's recreation. If you work at it, it's golf.

*Bob Hope*

The Foursome setting out from the first tee.

The General over-reaches his drive. His son has some difficulty in preserving an upright carriage.

The Quarry provides trouble for the General.

ANOTHER VETERAN FOURSOME.

THE COMBINED AGES OF PLAYERS AND CADDIES (THEIR SONS) TOTAL 867 YEARS.

The Rear-Admiral holes out into one of the Doctor's big prints.

The Bishop caught playing a slim game.

Return home. Late.

I only hit the ball about 220 off the tee, but I can always find it.

*Bonnie Lauer*

"Anyway it's better to break one's — clubs than to lose ones — temper!!"

The right way to play golf is to go up and hit the bloody thing.

*George Duncan*

"Wot are yer a-follerin 'im for Bill?"
"I'm going to listen to 'im play gowf!"

No matter what happens - never give up a hole. . . . In tossing in your cards after a bad beginning you also undermine your whole game, because to quit between tee and green is more habit-forming than drinking a highball before breakfast.

*Sam Snead*

10 A.M.     10.5     10.6     10.7

10.12     10.13     10.14     .0.15

## THE UNDRIVEN DRIVE.

A Story without words

10.20     10.21     10.17     10.27

10.28     10.29     10.30

I'm only scared of three things -
lightning, a side-hill putt, and
Ben Hogan.

*Sam Snead*

Pressure is going out there on the golf
course and thinking, 'If I don't do well,
I'll have to rob another bank.'

*Rick Meissner*
*(former touring pro & convicted bank robber)*

## VERY ADVANCED GOLF

IMPORTANT NOTICE (THE BALLOON HOLE). -PLAYERS ARE REQUESTED NOT TO ASCEND TO THE GREEN TILL THE PLAYERS IN FRONT HAVE QUITTED THE LADDER.

NEW MEMBER (*on Medal Day*). "Did you have a good round, Sir?"
SCRATCH PLAYER. "It would have been good, but I took six at that infernal fifth."
NEW MEMBER. "That's curious. I did much the same thing—a sixteen at that cursed fifteenth."

CADDIE (*as famous surgeon misses another short putt*). "Lummy! fancy bein' operated on by 'im!"

# A

**Notes**

Name

Address


Tel

Name

Address


Tel

Name

Address


Tel

Name

Address


Tel

## A

Name

Address


Tel

Name

Address


Tel

Name

Address


Tel

Name

Address


Tel

*Notes*

## B

Name

Address

Tel

Name

Address

Tel

Name

Address

Tel

Name

Address

Tel

*Notes*

## B

*Notes*

*Name*

*Address*

*Tel*

*Name*

*Address*

*Tel*

*Name*

*Address*

*Tel*

*Name*

*Address*

*Tel*

## C

**Notes**

Name

Address


Tel

Name

Address


Tel

Name

Address


Tel

Name

Address


Tel

# D

### Notes

Name

Address


Tel

Name

Address


Tel

Name

Address


Tel

Name

Address


Tel

## E

Name

Address


Tel

Name

Address


Tel

Name

Address


Tel

Name

Address


Tel

*Notes*

# E

**Notes**

Name

Address

Tel

---

Name

Address

Tel

---

Name

Address

Tel

---

Name

Address

Tel

## F

Name

Address


Tel

Name

Address


Tel

Name

Address


Tel

Name

Address


Tel

## Notes

# F

*Notes*

**Name**

**Address**

**Tel**

**Name**

**Address**

**Tel**

**Name**

**Address**

**Tel**

**Name**

**Address**

**Tel**

## G

**Name**

**Address**

**Tel**

**Name**

**Address**

**Tel**

**Name**

**Address**

**Tel**

**Name**

**Address**

**Tel**

*Notes*

# H

Name

Address

Tel

Name

Address

Tel

Name

Address

Tel

Name

Address

Tel

*Notes*

## I

**Name**

**Address**

**Tel**

**Name**

**Address**

**Tel**

**Name**

**Address**

**Tel**

**Name**

**Address**

**Tel**

*Notes*

## J

Name

Address

Tel

Name

Address

Tel

Name

Address

Tel

Name

Address

Tel

*Notes*

## K

Name

Address

Tel

Name

Address

Tel

Name

Address

Tel

Name

Address

Tel

*Notes*

# L

Name

Address

Tel

Name

Address

Tel

Name

Address

Tel

Name

Address

Tel

*Notes*

## M

Name

Address

Tel

Name

Address

Tel

Name

Address

Tel

Name

Address

Tel

*Notes*

# N

**Notes**

Name

Address

Tel

Name

Address

Tel

Name

Address

Tel

Name

Address

Tel

# O

Name

Address

Tel

Name

Address

Tel

Name

Address

Tel

Name

Address

Tel

*Notes*

# P

Name

Address

Tel

Name

Address

Tel

Name

Address

Tel

Name

Address

Tel

*Notes*

## Q

**Name**

**Address**

**Tel**

**Name**

**Address**

**Tel**

**Name**

**Address**

**Tel**

**Name**

**Address**

**Tel**

*Notes*

R

Notes

Name

Address


Tel

Name

Address


Tel

Name

Address


Tel

Name

Address


Tel

## S

Notes

Name
Address

Tel

Name
Address

Tel

Name
Address

Tel

Name
Address

Tel

## S

**Name**

**Address**


**Tel**

**Name**

**Address**


**Tel**

**Name**

**Address**


**Tel**

**Name**

**Address**


**Tel**

*Notes*

# T

**Name**

**Address**

**Tel**

**Name**

**Address**

**Tel**

**Name**

**Address**

**Tel**

**Name**

**Address**

**Tel**

## Notes

*T*

*Name*

*Address*

*Tel*

*Name*

*Address*

*Tel*

*Name*

*Address*

*Tel*

*Name*

*Address*

*Tel*

*Notes*

# U

Name

Address

Tel

Name

Address

Tel

Name

Address

Tel

Name

Address

Tel

## Notes

# V

*Notes*

**Name**

**Address**

**Tel**

**Name**

**Address**

**Tel**

**Name**

**Address**

**Tel**

**Name**

**Address**

**Tel**

# W

Name

Address

Tel

Name

Address

Tel

Name

Address

Tel

Name

Address

Tel

*Notes*

....................

....................

....................

....................

....................

....................

....................

....................

....................

....................

....................

....................

....................

....................

# W

**Notes**

Name

Address

Tel

Name

Address

Tel

Name

Address

Tel

Name

Address

Tel

## XYZ

Name

Address


Tel

Name

Address


Tel

Name

Address


Tel

Name

Address


Tel

## Notes

# XYZ

Name

Address

Tel

Name

Address

Tel

Name

Address

Tel

Name

Address

Tel

## Notes